Praise for CEO Chef

"Jim Connolly has created a breakthrough with Cooking Team Building 2.0. This book delivers practical strategies that not only strengthen teamwork but also drive measurable sales results—a must-read for every business leader."

—Eric Lofholm, Best-Selling Author of The System
Master Sales Trainer

"This book proves that leadership is best learned by doing—and doing together. The cooking metaphor is powerful, practical, and fun."

—Sidrid Rivera, Life & Business Coach,
Best-Selling Author of Be You

"Jim Connolly is a rare corporate team builder. In his latest book, Corporate Team Building 2.0, he refines and expands on his proven formula—one that is uniquely fun, practical, and effective.

His approach transforms team building into a hands-on experience by using cooking as the foundation. As individuals collaborate to prepare a delicious meal, they learn to become more effective in the workplace. The cooking process becomes a powerful metaphor: just as diverse ingredients must be blended into harmony, so too must corporate individuals come together to create a productive, motivated, and cohesive team.

Along the way, participants laugh, learn, and discover new sides of one another in fresh and unexpected ways. The result is not just a stronger team, but one that communicates better, trusts more deeply, and produces lasting results.

If you want to boost corporate productivity while giving your team an unforgettable experience, call on Jim Connolly."

—Tommy Lemonade, President of Tommy's Lemonade, Creator of Lemonade Sensations

"Working with CEO Chef, our business college staff team learned to collaborate and engage more effectively to reach our goals. CEO Chef visited our campus and helped us demonstrate, both through our cooking skills and outside of our usual work environment, that there is nothing we can't accomplish. It has been a great reflection of our strength-building program and a wonderful addition to our ongoing efforts."

—Ken Rappe| California State University, Northridge

"CEO Chef is very professional and easy to work with. The advantages of your program include its easy implementation across various locations, consistently meeting team objectives, and being highly engaging."

—Noel Rettig, Ed.D| Vice President, Organizational Effectiveness & Learning, Fire & Rain

"For organizations that want to see their staff work as a team to resolve a problem, your presentation laid the groundwork. It then became each team's task to plan, attack, and conclude with impressive results.

Your ability to tailor the presentation and event to our expectations was exceptional. Our group has heard every type of motivational and management speaker available. Your service introduces a refreshing change to the training world."

—Stephen Farrell |Regional Administration
Howard Hughes Medical Institute

"Thanks so much for your flexibility and help. Our teams are much better for the exercise, and I was amazed at how much it loosened everyone up and took us to a new level in terms of openness with each other.

Thanks so much for everything!!!!!"

—Amgen

"We wanted some enhancement in taking them out of their comfort zone, and that's what CEO Chef did for us. They've been great to work with; Jim's a great motivator and speaker. Renee has been excellent working with my staff. We will definitely use these folks (CEO Chef) again in the near future."

—SCE |Risk Management Group Team Building Offsite

"We really enjoyed the Competitive Chef competition! CEO Chef was able to handle our large group of 180 restaurant managers effortlessly. Our managers were introduced to new recipes and creative ways of cooking and are still discussing the experience. CEO Chef took care of all the details. It was a worry-free event for us."

—Laurie H. | Director of Training,
Apple American Group

"We have 380 Bosch people at an event to bring everyone together. CEO Chef put on a great event for us, and Jim was a wonderful host. The food was fabulous and we couldn't believe that we did it all ourselves!"

—Bosch Security and Bosch Communications Sales Retreat

"Bonding and dealing with the uncertainty and issues of not having a kitchen gave us an opportunity to communicate, support each other, and work as a team. It was inspiring to see how we collectively made a great meal that everyone enjoyed."

—Diageo Leadership Retreat

"We had 100 attendees at our all-staff retreat. I found CEO Chef, and we couldn't have been more pleased with their process. We didn't realize what we were capable of doing when we came together as a team. We had such a great time, enjoyed some great food, and now we know that if we could do this, we can do anything asked of us at the workplace!

So I fully endorse CEO Chef!"

—Rio Hondo College

"We are working with our HR team to build a program focused on stretching our strengths and enabling us to achieve anything we set our minds to... CEO Chef has come out here to help us demonstrate—through our cooking skills—that even though none of us are chefs, there is nothing we can't accomplish!"

—Cornerstone School

"CEO Chef tailored our HR offsite goals to their culinary team-building experience. It really brought us together, and we left with the understanding that if we can do this cooking challenge here, we can accomplish much more as a new project team!"

—Rabobank | Leadership and Team Building Offsite

"As Senior Vice President of Human Resources at Discovery and formerly Senior Vice President of NBC/Universal, I have worked with CEO Chef many times before and had great experiences at NBC/Universal. I led an event tonight with my new team, and we enjoyed it tremendously. I highly recommend this for anyone doing team building events."

—Discovery Communications (Channel) | Leadership Offsite

"... I'd like to add my endorsement of CEO Chef, we are building a program here with our HR team on stretching your strengths and to be able to accomplish anything you want ... CEO Chef has been able to come out here and help us prove though our cooking skills, even though none of us are cooks, that there is nothing we can't accomplish, so it's been a great mirror to our strength building program and a great compliment to what we are trying to accomplish."

—National University

"I am president of N-Able Alliance. I work with corporate executives and their teams. Today, we had CEO Chef come here in Dallas to work with one of my best customers, Nokia. Jim and the CEO Chef team did an outstanding job, and we achieved everything we set out to do and more. I thoroughly recommend them to anyone who is thinking of doing this kind of event."

—Nokia Leadership Conference

"We just had our first Arden "Iron Chef" event hosted by CEO Chef. It was a fantastic, well-organized event that was lots of fun, promoted team building, and was overall a great experience. Thank you so much, CEO Chef. Everyone had a wonderful time."

—Arden Realty Annual Team Bonding Event

"As a senior leader at Southern California Edison, it was essential to bring in a top-tier training organization that could make a difference with the project team I was hosting at our leadership offsite. From my sources, I was able to find CEO Chef, Mr. Jim Connolly, for this project and several others. His team did an excellent job of providing wonderful team-building services through cooking and became our go-to program to help our project teams get on track and understand how to maximize their potential. It's great, and I believe you'll be very satisfied with the services they offer."

—SCE | Leadership Offsite

"The CEO Chef activity was a huge success! People couldn't stop talking about it... Thanks so much for your flexibility and help. Our teams are much better for the exercise, and I was amazed at how much it loosened everyone up and elevated us to a new level of openness. Thank you for everything!

...we worked with CEO Chef to team build with our two sales teams and found it to be an extraordinary experience—fun and full of valuable lessons about teamwork. It's a great example of communication, planning, organization, and, most importantly, just having fun and learning more about each other. So, thank you, CEO Chef!"

—Amgen | Sales Team Training

"I love the program today and in over 30 years in the industry in sales, this the <u>best</u> by far!"

"I am not so athletic, and I am sick of doing athletic events at these team-building events. And it was the first time I could enjoy cooking and eating while building team spirit as well. It was awesome! I would highly recommend it!"

—Blue Shield Insurance | Team Building Sales Workshop

"We wanted a chance to get to know each other, be comfortable, and have fun, and that's exactly what it did. It helped us work better as a team!

I thought this adventure we took was awesome, and we got to know each other a little better. We were able to work together as a team and have a great time doing it.

I would recommend it to anyone considering hiring Jim (Connolly) and CEO Chef."

—SCE | "TAPS" Leadership Offsite

COOKING TEAM BUILDING
2.0
REWIRING THE WAY TEAMS CONNECT, PERFORM, AND SUCCEED

"Cook, Connect, Transform"

Dr. Renee Gordon

Jim Connolly

Foreword by
Eric Lofholm

© 2025 Dr. Renee Gordon & Jim Connolly

Published by:
Wisdom Eye Publishing
Chattanooga, TN
www.WisdomEyePublishing.com

All Rights Reserved. No part of this book may be used or reproduced in any manner whatsoever without the expressed written permission of the author. Address all inquiries to:
Jim Connolly
www.ceochef.com

All efforts have been made to source all quotes accurately. CEO Chef Consulting can invite the authors to your live event. For more information or to book an event, visit CEO Chef Consulting at:
www.CEOChef.com or www.CEOChefConsulting.com

ISBN: 979-8-9896108-4-6

Printed in the United States of America

Disclaimer

The purpose of this book is to educate and entertain. Neither the author nor the publisher guarantees that anyone following the ideas, tips, suggestions, techniques, or strategies within it will become successful. The author and publisher shall have neither liability nor responsibility to anyone with respect to any loss or damage caused, or alleged to be caused, directly or indirectly, by the information contained in this book.

DEDICATION

Dedicated to the leaders and teams who turn collaboration into culture and culture into success.

ACKNOWLEDGEMENTS:
IT TAKES A TEAM

Writing this book has been a journey of collaboration—fitting, since collaboration is its very heartbeat. I am deeply grateful to the many leaders, managers, and employees I have had the privilege of working with over the years. Your willingness to open up, take risks, and learn together has been both my inspiration and my classroom.

To the organizations that invited me into their kitchens and boardrooms, thank you for trusting me to guide your teams through the experience of cooking and connecting. Every story, every laugh, and every breakthrough moment shaped the insights within these pages.

To my wife, partner, and co-author, Dr. Renee, your love, wisdom, and belief in this vision have been my constant source of encouragement. None of this would be possible without your steady presence and partnership in life and business.

And to the countless teams who rolled up their sleeves, chopped, stirred, and plated more than meals—you helped prove that food is one of the most powerful tools for building culture. This book is as much yours as it is mine.

INTRODUCTION: WHERE CULTURE MEETS THE CUTTING BOARD

In boardrooms worldwide, executives are looking for more than just improved meetings—they're looking for moments that transform teams, foster alignment, and cultivate trust that endures beyond the next quarter. The stakes are high: disengaged employees, hybrid fatigue, and the increasing expectation that leaders must shape not only business outcomes but also human connection.

This is where *Cooking Team Building 2.0* comes into play.

This is not merely a book about cooking. It is a strategic manual for leveraging culinary collaboration to inspire cultural breakthroughs. Grounded in twenty-five years of field-tested leadership development, this guide introduces you to the TAC™ Framework—an actionable, experience-driven model that is redefining how organizations foster cohesion, performance, and emotional intelligence from the inside out.

Inside, you'll discover how executive-level team building can advance beyond icebreakers and into immersive, meaningful engagement. You'll see why the shared experience of creating a meal can unlock leadership behaviors, reveal communication patterns, and foster authentic trust across levels and departments. You'll also find a blueprint for incorporating these insights into scalable, sustainable change, whether you lead a sales force, an HR department, or the entire company.

This book is intended for serious leaders who recognize that culture isn't created by chance—and who are prepared to explore an unexpected yet profoundly effective approach to shaping it.

Let's step into the kitchen and embrace a new kind of leadership.

FOREWORD

When I first heard about Cooking Team Building, I was curious. Since I've dedicated my career to teaching sales and leadership systems, I understand that success doesn't happen by chance. It comes from following a proven method. Jim Connolly has developed exactly that—a consistent, results-driven system for strengthening teams through one of our most powerful and shared experiences: cooking.

Here's what makes this book and this approach so valuable. Most team-building activities are fun in the moment, but they don't last. I've seen it with sales teams, executive teams, and everywhere in between: people get excited for a day, then it's back to business as usual. What Jim and Dr. Renee Gordon have created is different. It's not just about morale—it's about transformation. It's about rewiring how people trust, communicate, and perform together.

Cooking Team Building 2.0 introduces the TAC™ Framework—Team → Action → Culture. This isn't just an idea; it's a system. Systems are what create predictable, repeatable success. In my world of sales training, the right system can help someone double or triple their income. In Jim's world of leadership and culture, the right system can help companies save millions, retain their best talent, and unlock their people's potential.

As you'll discover in these pages, the kitchen is the ideal learning environment. When time is limited, titles fade away. Egos take a backseat to teamwork. Leadership appears naturally. And when people share that genuine experience together, they won't forget it. They carry it back to the office, the boardroom, and their clients.

If you're a CEO, HR leader, or department head, you already know the truth: your team is capable of more. This book shows you how to unlock that potential. Use it. Apply it. Share it. And if you get the chance, don't just read the book—experience Cooking Team Building live. Because, like in sales, knowledge isn't enough. It's action that delivers results.

Jim and Renee have passed along the recipe. Now it's your turn to step into the kitchen and guide your team to the next level.

—Eric Lofholm, Best-Selling Author of *The System*

Master Sales Trainer

PREFACE

If you're holding this book, you're likely a leader who knows one thing for sure: **your team is capable of more.**

More connection.

More collaboration.

More trust.

More results.

But here's the truth that most leadership books won't tell you— **you can't teach teamwork by talking about it.** You have to create an environment where people *live it, feel it,* and *experience it together*. That's where the kitchen comes in.

For the last 28 years, I've been leading Cooking Team Building programs for some of the world's top companies—Google, Facebook, Stanford, Kaiser Permanente—along with plenty of mid-sized firms and local organizations that care just as deeply about their people. What I've seen time and time again is this: **when people cook together, walls come down and real teamwork starts to sizzle.**

This book is the upgraded edition of my original *Cooking Team Building* framework. It's sharpened by decades of hands-on experience and packed with the lessons, insights, and behind-the-scenes strategies that turn a simple cooking event into a full-blown leadership accelerator.

You won't find fluffy theory here. What you will find are real stories, practical takeaways, and proven methods you can apply—whether you're an HR leader, team facilitator, sales director, or CEO.

And this book is not the end of the story. It's the launch pad. Hot on its heels is my follow-up companion guide, *21 Ways to Cook Up Company Culture*. That book delivers the daily strategies—the practical moves you and your team can make to build and reinforce the culture you care about most.

Leadership isn't taught in lecture halls. It's forged in real moments, with real people, under real pressure. That's what the kitchen gives us. That's what this book gives you.

Now, sharpen your knives—and your leadership mindset.

It's time to cook.

—Jim Connolly

Founder & President of CEO Chef

HOW TO USE THIS BOOK

Cooking Team Building 2.0 isn't meant to be read once and put on a shelf. It's designed to work like a well-used kitchen tool—reliable, accessible, and always within reach when you need it most.

Here's how to get the most out of it:

Read a Chapter. Reflect. Apply.

Each chapter is built around a core lesson pulled straight from real Cooking Team Building experiences.

At the end of every chapter, you'll find two key elements:

- **Takeaway Recipe**: A quick summary of the leadership insight or team-building principle you just learned.

- **Time to Stir It Up**: Thought-provoking questions to help you reflect, personalize, and bring the lesson back to your workplace.

Use these sections to spark internal discussions, coaching conversations, or small-group training.

Use It As a Leadership Toolbox

This isn't a book you have to read cover to cover in one sitting. You can open to any chapter and use it to:

- Kick off a leadership meeting
- Train a new manager
- Reinforce a team-building session

- Plan your next off-site or retreat
- Shift a stale culture into one that thrives

👥 Involve Your Team

The best results come when teams read and work through this together. Give a copy to your department leads, HR partners, or executive team. Use the chapter reflections to guide honest conversations. *That's where the magic happens.*

🔄 Pair It with the Companion Book

Once you've explored the bigger picture of leadership and transformation through this book, grab a copy of my follow-up, *21 Ways to Cook Up Company Culture*. It's the daily habits version of this book—short, practical, actionable tips to build culture week after week.

📞 Ready to Go Deeper?

This book is just one part of a larger experience. If you want to bring a live Cooking Team Building event to your company or explore what it would look like to use this approach at scale, reach out. That's where the real transformation begins.

You can connect with me at **CEOChef.com**

Keep this book close. Use it often. And remember, **great teams aren't born; they're built… sometimes in a kitchen.**

Let's get cooking.

—Jim

🔥 Ready to Take the Next Step?

You are about to experience the leadership power of *Cooking Team Building 2.0*. When you're ready to bring this energy into your organization—or help your team live these lessons every day—here's where to go next:

📖 Coming Soon!

21 Ways to Cook Up Company Culture

The perfect companion to this book—a quick-action guide packed with 21 practical strategies to strengthen communication, collaboration, and trust across your team.

Use it with your leaders. Share it with your HR team. Build culture daily, not just at events.

▶ Available on Amazon and CEOChef.com

🍴 Bring the Experience to Your Team

Want to turn these pages into a real-world experience?

Book a **live Cooking Team Building program** for your next leadership retreat, sales meeting, or culture kickoff.

- ✔ Onsite & offsite options
- ✔ Customized to your team goals
- ✔ High-impact, unforgettable, and results-driven

✱ **Visit CEOChef.com** or email *info@ceochef.com* to schedule your session.

✒ Thinking About Writing a Book of Your Own?

Your book should work as hard as you do. I help speakers, coaches, and business owners write and publish books that grow their credibility, brand, and revenue.

You don't need to be a writer. You need the right strategy.

🔑 Let's talk about how your book can open doors.

⬇ Visit FastBookPublishing.com or connect with me on LinkedIn: *Jim Connolly, CEO Chef*

Let's keep the momentum going. You're just getting started.

CONTENTS

Executive Summary 25

Chapter 1: The Broken Blueprint of Team Building 29

Chapter 2: What Defines a Great Team? 35

Chapter 3: Introducing TAC™ – Team Associative Conditioning 40

Chapter 4: Why Cooking? 53

Chapter 5: Creating the Ultimate Cooking Team Building Experience 60

Chapter 6: The Hidden Heat Behind High-Performance Teams 66

Chapter 7: The Mechanics of Connection 73

Chapter 8: The Neuroscience of Flavor and Performance 82

Chapter 9: The Future of Work — Why TAC™ Is the Cultural Model of the 2030s 91

Chapter 10: Creating Leaders to Build Teams: Becoming the Leader You're Meant to Be 99

Chapter 11: Executive Cooking — Boardroom-Ready Leadership in the Kitchen 106

Chapter 12: Implementation Models of TAC™ 114

Chapter 13: The Executive Playbook — Scaling TAC™ Across Your Enterprise 120

Chapter 14: Now Take Action—Bring the Heat Beyond the Kitchen 126

Appendix A - Mini Resource 129

Appendix B - Team Building Comparison Chart 132

Appendix C - Various Cooking Team Building Themes 133

Appendix D - The CTB 2.0 Implementation Toolkit 135

Appendix F - FAQ 138

EXECUTIVE SUMMARY

THE CULTURE ADVANTAGE YOU CAN'T AFFORD TO IGNORE

The strength of a culture is not defined by values displayed on the wall, but by the behaviors exhibited in the hall.

-Author Unknown

Today's leaders face unprecedented challenges from hybrid teams, talent retention, generational changes, and the increasing need for meaningful workplace connections. Traditional team-building and leadership development methods no longer suffice. What's needed now is **a comprehensive, experiential, and emotionally intelligent approach to shaping culture.**

Cooking Team Building 2.0 provides a solution by combining hands-on culinary experiences with the **TAC™ framework** (Team→ Action→ Culture), a system designed to build trust, enhance leadership, and improve performance through culture.

This book presents a strong argument for why the kitchen could be your next competitive advantage—and how Cooking Team Building can change team dynamics quickly, in just hours instead of months.

What You'll See at a Glance

- **Why Cooking?**

It's a hands-on, high-pressure environment where roles blur, trust forms quickly, and collaboration feels natural rather than just theoretical.

- **The Neuroscience Behind the Method.**
- Sensory learning—taste, smell, and touch—activates oxytocin and dopamine, forming memory anchors that strengthen emotional bonds and enhance recall.
- **Leadership in Action.**
- Cooking together showcases leadership readiness, emotional intelligence, adaptability, and teamwork under pressure in real time.
- **From One-Day to Ongoing Impact.**
- The book introduces the **TAC™ process**, a scalable roadmap that begins with a powerful cooking experience and extends into coaching, leadership development, and organizational design.
- **Customization at Every Level.**
- From the boardroom to frontline teams, we develop engagements that align with your business goals, leadership challenges, and industry context.

Why This Matters to You as a Decision-Maker?

- **For the CEO**: Align the company culture with strategic goals. Achieve results by focusing on behavioral change rather than just changing policies.
- **For the CHRO**: Reduce attrition and boost engagement with a people-first, scalable approach rooted in psychological safety.
- **For the VP of Sales or Ops**: Improve team dynamics, break down silos, and promote high-trust collaboration effectively and accurately.

- **For event planners**: Craft a memorable experience that aligns with your brand, going beyond entertainment to deliver tangible business results.

Why It Works?

Unlike passive seminars or theoretical workshops, Cooking Team Building promotes **hands-on learning** that sticks because people **experience it, connect with it, and remember it**.

It's more than just a team-building event.

It's a **trust booster**. It's more than just a leadership simulation.

It's a **cultural model**.

Cooking Team Building 2.0 acts as a blueprint for developing high-trust, high-performance teams—starting in the kitchen and expanding throughout your organization.

Are you prepared to lead in a new way?

You don't have to make a full change today, but you should start gaining momentum.

We invite you to:

- **Schedule a Culinary Team Experience** for your upcoming leadership retreat or off-site event.
- **Schedule a Discovery Call** with our team to align your cultural vision with the TAC™ model.
- **Request our Corporate Guide** to learn how companies like yours have changed leadership and culture—one meal at a time.

Culture is no longer just an HR initiative; it's a leadership decision. The best time to act is before your competitors do.

Let's create a culture that draws in top talent and keeps them engaged.

CHAPTER 1

THE BROKEN BLUEPRINT OF TEAM BUILDING

"Tell me and I forget, teach me and I may remember, involve me and I learn."

—*Benjamin Franklin*

Chapter Highlights

- Learn why traditional team-building activities often fail to create lasting changes or cultural shifts.

- Explore how Cooking Team Building 2.0 offers a revolutionary approach based on behavioral science and emotional intelligence.

- Discover how the TAC™ (Team Associative Conditioning) method transforms team dynamics through practical metaphors and proven collaboration.

- Learn how a high-pressure kitchen environment can foster lasting leadership lessons and boost team trust.

- See how the multisensory cooking experience can foster emotional bonds and transform temporary engagement into lasting behavior change.

Imagine this—It's 7:00 PM on a Saturday. The restaurant is packed. The kitchen is running at full capacity. Orders are coming in every 30 seconds. Then—disaster strikes. The head chef is out sick, the sous chef just overcooked the steak for a VIP guest, and my line cooks are looking at me, waiting for a solution. What happens next will determine whether this night ends in chaos or flawless service.

The truth is: *"That night, I learned a powerful lesson: A great team doesn't panic. A great team doesn't blame. A great team executes because they trust each other and understand their roles. And that's exactly what I teach companies today through TAC™."*

We've tried everything—escape rooms, trust falls, and even goat yoga. It's fun at the moment, but nothing really changes.

If that sounds familiar, you're not alone.

In the boardrooms of Fortune 500 companies and the conference rooms of rapidly growing firms, HR leaders, training directors, and department heads all share a common frustration: **team-building events just don't have lasting effects.**

They boost your team's energy for a few hours, maybe a day.

But by the next week, the same communication problems return. Silos remain. Engagement stays fragile. And your team is still far from working as a unified group.

You're not doing anything wrong; **you're just following a flawed plan.**

The True Story Behind Traditional Team Building

Team-building has grown into a busy industry filled with icebreakers, offsites, and improv games. While the goal is positive, the results often don't justify the time and money invested.

Let's be honest: most traditional team-building methods aim for **temporary excitement** rather **than lasting transformation**.

They focus on entertainment rather than endurance.

Here's why they fall short:

- They are out of touch with the real workplace dynamic.
- They don't talk about emotional safety, trust, or communication when they're under pressure.
- They rarely align with the company's leadership style or cultural goals.
- They form superficial relationships without any behavioral reinforcement.
- And worst of all, there's no way to turn the experience into real results.

A Quick Comparison: What You've Tried Versus What Works

Experience Type	Immediate Fun	Real-World Transfer	Leadership Development	Emotional Anchor	Lasting Impact
Escape Rooms	✅	❌	❌	❌	❌
Ropes Courses	✅	❌	❌	❌	❌
Improv Nights	✅	❌	❌	❌	❌
Cooking Team Building 2.0	✅	✅	✅	✅	✅

So, what's the alternative?

You need more than just an event.

You require a **system** rooted in behavioral psychology, emotional intelligence, and multi-sensory engagement. It should be something your team not only enjoys but also remembers, applies, and discusses for months (and meetings) to come.

That's precisely what *Cooking Team Building 2.0* is designed to achieve.

At its core, there's a framework called **TAC™ – Team Associative Conditioning**. This unique approach not only involves your team but also changes how they think, communicate, and support each other.

How?

Not by telling them what to do or handing out trust bracelets, but by placing them in a real-world setting—**the kitchen**—and challenging them to create something complex, meaningful, and high-stakes together.

No recipes.

No titles.

No roadmap.

Just each other, the tools before them, and the pressure to perform—not as individuals, but as a team.

And when it works (and it always does), it shifts something profound. It anchors behavior, opens new channels of respect and creativity, and sparks something traditional team-building can't reach: **emotional buy-in.**

In this book, you'll learn:

- Why Most Team-Building Efforts Fail and How to Avoid the Trap
- The science behind TAC™ and its application to your business
- How cooking connects to memory, emotion, leadership, and learning
- What Great Teams Do Differently—and How to Build Your Own
- And how to use this system to enhance relationships at every level of your organization, from the C-suite to the kitchen staff.

If you've ever wondered how to transform your team from disconnected to unstoppable, this book is for you.

Let's stop fooling around. Let's begin creating something meaningful.

Takeaway Recipe

A savory summary of what matters most.

Chapter 1 highlights the limits of traditional team-building methods that often entertain but rarely transform. It shows the critical gap between short-term excitement and long-term impact—and introduces TAC™, a approach that changes how teams think, work together, and lead. By placing professionals in a kitchen without titles, scripts, or recipes, TAC™ sparks real teamwork under pressure, turning performance into practice. This chapter sets the stage for why Cooking Team Building 2.0 is more than just an event—it's a strategic system for building trust, accountability, and cultural alignment in high-performing organizations.

Time to Stir It Up

Questions to keep the ideas simmering.

1. Think about your latest team-building activity—what, if anything, was different afterward? Why do you think those changes (or no changes) occurred?

2. How can your team benefit from a shared experience that mimics real-world pressure while building trust and communication?

3. What will it require for your organization to move from "fun" to genuine transformation in your team development strategy?

CHAPTER 2

WHAT DEFINES A GREAT TEAM?

"Unity is strength... when there is teamwork and collaboration, wonderful things can be achieved."

— *Mattie Stepanek*

Chapter Highlights

- What are the essential components that turn a group of individuals into a high-performing team?

- How do values like trust, communication, and commitment foster organizational excellence?

- This chapter explores the six key qualities that support world-class teams, illustrated through lively, real-world stories from business and culinary leadership.

- Discover how embracing collaboration, diverse perspectives, and leadership can foster synergy, drive innovation, and generate sustainable results.

Building the DNA of a great team

Every high-performing team surpasses the combined efforts of its members. Exceptional teams foster synergy—where collaboration, trust, and commitment turn ordinary work into outstanding results.

Reflecting on the Golden State Warriors 'championship wins, it's clear that outstanding performance comes from values like respect, fun, and focus—not just individual talent. Their success wasn't based on stars playing alone but on a strong team spirit. The same applies to modern organizations: teamwork beats working alone.

Let's examine six key traits that define a truly great team.

1. Communication: The Gateway to Understanding

Communication extends beyond words; it's about connection. From workplace strategies to ordering food in a new language, communication is most effective when it's based on intention and empathy—even if it's imperfect.

Understanding styles (Visual, Auditory, Kinesthetic) helps leaders prevent miscommunication and promote inclusive dialogue. Great teams clarify, listen actively, and continually strive to understand others' perspectives. A shared "language" of understanding builds trust, loyalty, and effectiveness.

Lesson: When uncertain, ask for clarification—because perspective affects how we see reality.

2. Collaboration: Where Ideas Thrive

True teamwork starts when ego steps aside. Teams succeed when members concentrate on common goals rather than personal fame.

Whether designing a menu or launching a new product, collaboration transforms pressure into opportunity. One chef's change—inviting the kitchen team to share ideas—unlocked new creativity and built a stronger, more engaged team.

Lesson: Collaborating often surpasses individual talent.

3. Cooperation: The Key to Unlocking Synergy

Cooperation merges differences into harmony. Like ingredients in a great soup, each team member provides unique value. Alone, they are capable; together, through deliberate and steady integration, they become exceptional.

In business, just like in the kitchen, teamwork fuels momentum, engagement, and improved results. One plus one can equal three—when synergy exists.

Lesson: Purposeful collaboration increases effectiveness.

4. Commitment: Going All In

There's a difference between involvement and commitment. Commitment means taking ownership—diving in wholeheartedly, even when unsure.

A new head chef learned this firsthand: when he stopped "trying" and started "being" the leader, everything changed. Committed teams work with clarity and purpose. They take ownership of their roles, lift each other up, and stay aligned with the mission.

Lesson: Commitment is infectious and essential.

5. Trust: The Foundation of Team Growth

Trust isn't built overnight or through a single event. It's earned every day—by acting, listening, and releasing control.

In team-building workshops, the well-known "trust fall" might represent the idea, but real trust builds over time. It requires vulnerability and confidence that your team will back you up—especially when problems come up.

Lesson: Trust transforms micromanagement into empowerment.

6. Leadership: The Listening Edge

Leadership isn't about titles — it's about being attentive. Great leaders don't just give directions; they listen, seek input, and build consensus.

One restaurateur learned this lesson before Valentine's Day service. By following his dishwashers' suggestions, he achieved a quicker, more efficient dinner rush—and boosted guest satisfaction and team morale.

Lesson: Leaders don't need to know everything — they just have to listen more effectively than anyone else.

Takeaway Recipe

World-class teams aren't created by accident—they're intentionally built through communication and care. When the six team traits—communication, collaboration, cooperation, commitment, trust, and leadership—are cultivated and practiced, teams become resilient, innovative, and high-performing.

Whether you're running a kitchen or a business, the core principles remain the same: your people are your greatest asset. Empower them with clarity, connection, and culture—and you'll achieve more than just success. You'll create significance.

Time to Stir It Up

Questions to keep the ideas simmering.

1. Which of the six team characteristics is currently the strongest in your organization? Which one requires the most development?

2. How can you effectively show commitment or trust to your team?

3. How can your organization intentionally encourage moments of collaboration, perspective-sharing, and feedback?

CHAPTER 3

INTRODUCING TAC™ – TEAM ASSOCIATIVE CONDITIONING

"A great team doesn't panic. A great team doesn't blame. A great team executes—because they trust each other and know their roles."

— *Jim Connolly, CEO Chef*

Chapter Highlights

- Discover why traditional team-building often fails to create lasting impacts in the workplace—and how TAC™ bridges that crucial gap.

- Discover what Team Associative Conditioning (TAC™) is and why it depends on neuroscience, sensory learning, and emotional engagement.

- Explore the five key pillars of TAC™—trust, adaptability, communication, action, and accountability—using clear real-world examples.

- See how TAC™ not only encourages good behavior in the moment but also helps develop new habits that transform team dynamics long after the experience ends.

- Understand how cooking is more than just an activity — it serves as a metaphor for leadership, culture, and high performance that transforms.

There's a reason most team-building activities don't translate to the workplace.

It's not because the event wasn't fun or the facilitator wasn't good; it's because the event lacked a real **connection.**

A link between *moments* and *missions*. Between *action* and *application*. Between *excitement* and *resilience*.

That bridge represents TAC™—Team Associative Conditioning.

What Is TAC™?

Team Associative Conditioning (TAC™) is a behavior-anchoring process that employs multisensory experiences—sight, sound, smell, taste, and emotional cues—to foster lasting new team dynamics.

It's more than merely a team-building tool.

It's a **framework for transformation**.

TAC™ leverages our expertise in neuroscience, emotional learning, and leadership behavior—transforming it into practical application through immersive, collective experiences that foster genuine, lasting change.

Where most programs focus on what your team knows, TAC™ emphasizes what they *feel, internalize, and use.*

The Science of Sensory Anchoring

Studies show that we retain:

- 10% of what we hear
- 20% of what we read
- But **up to 80% of what we experience physically and emotionally.**

That's why **associative learning**—the link between a new behavior and a sensory or emotional trigger—is so powerful.

In cooking, each step provides an opportunity to learn.

- The heat of a challenge
- The pressure of time
- The joy of collaborating together
- The smell of everything blending smoothly.

Connecting learning to the senses enhances memory. Linking memory to action promotes behavior change. When behavior shifts within a team, **culture also shifts.**

That's TAC™ in action.

The Four+ Pillars of TAC™

Let's examine the key skills your team develops through this model — *both theoretically and practically.*

- **1. Trust and Transparency**

Trust isn't established in meetings; it's fostered through small moments.

- When a team member continues where another left off
- When someone admits they don't know something and receives support instead of shame.
- When feedback is given without ego

Cooking together creates these moments in real-time.

Initially, building trust can be challenging. A common tendency is to over-control, often called "micro-managing." However, trust is essential for full participation in our culinary team exercises, and it's a valuable lesson participants carry back to the workplace for application.

However, the trust we're talking about is built more on daily choices. This trust relies on knowing your team well and believing in their success by allowing them to think, imagine, and accomplish the final results of their projects. So, it mainly boils down to communication and maintaining an ongoing conversation with each member to keep that trust.

Trust is built through consistency. In business, trust isn't gained by grand gestures or isolated moments; it's fostered through small, repeated actions that demonstrate reliability, transparency, and respect over time. Whether it's a leader keeping promises, a team member communicating openly, or an organization staying true to its values under pressure, trust naturally emerges from consistent behavior. With trust, teams work more efficiently, collaborate better, and innovate without fear. Without it, even the most talented individuals hesitate, second-guess, and eventually disengage. Ultimately, trust isn't just a soft skill—it's the foundation supporting every measurable result in business performance.

A lack of trust creates a major fault line in any organization.

When you can't rely on your team—or your team can't rely on you—that's not just a small crack in the foundation; it's the start of a complete breakdown.

In a professional kitchen, trust is an unspoken language. Everyone working behind the hot line knows instinctively that **anything behind the hot line is assumed to be hot.** There's no second-guessing or hesitation. In an environment where every second counts, you trust your training and your team. You trust that every pot, every sauté pan, and every surface near the heat must be handled carefully—always with a dry kitchen towel—because even one lapse could cause injury or disrupt the service rhythm.

In contrast, you expect the preparation areas—like the butcher's table—to be cool or cold to the touch. This is a key distinction. Now, imagine if someone, either unaware or careless, left a sizzling hot stainless steel pan in the middle of the prep area. One misplaced item, one broken protocol. Suddenly, a team member gets burned, trust is broken, and the smooth flow of a busy kitchen comes to a halt.

The same principle applies to business.

When trust and transparency break down, even small breaches can weaken confidence, cause hesitation, and disrupt the momentum and performance that your organization relies on. Without trust, progress stalls. Communication diminishes. Results decline.

Trust isn't a luxury; it's the foundation that keeps everything operating smoothly.

Real-World Results: Trust Established Without a Word

During a cooking team experience, a junior team member accidentally burned a key component of the dish. Instead of blaming her, her teammates supported her. One adjusted the recipe, and another offered to switch tasks. No one barked orders—because everyone took ownership of the moment together. That single act of trust changed their daily interactions.

- **2. Adaptability and Innovation**

What happens when a team realizes halfway through the event that a key ingredient is missing?

They innovate.

They adapt. They focus on what's possible.

In business and cooking, the result of a recipe is never certain.

Adaptability is frequently the key to innovation.

One Sunday evening during the early service, we faced an unexpected challenge: we didn't have enough specialty items to satisfy the demand for our daily featured dishes.

Typically, even when we received late Saturday deliveries, Sunday deliveries were rare. The night before, our Saturday specials had flown out of the kitchen faster than expected. By Sunday, we were left with just six orders of venison and six orders of ivory salmon from Alaska—far too few to cover an entire evening's service. Our guests had come to expect wild game and a unique seafood specialty, and a handful of portions simply wasn't enough.

What can we do?

Through adaptability and a willingness to innovate under pressure, we found the solution. Instead of serving full-sized portions of each entrée, we cut the six portions of salmon and venison in half. This gave us twelve smaller servings of each. To improve the experience further, we paired them with the last twelve portions of Beluga caviar, a specialty soup course, and a cappuccino soufflé for dessert.

Thus, our **Special Sunday Supper** was created.

Originally created out of necessity, the new tasting-style menu **sold out by the end of the night**. The response was so overwhelmingly positive that we decided to make it a weekly tradition. What was once our most inconsistent service of the week quickly started to rival Friday and Saturday nights.

We not only revitalized Sunday service but also added a profitable evening for our wait staff, significantly increasing our overall margins.

Adaptability fosters innovation. Innovation opens doors to opportunity. And opportunity fuels growth."
-Jim Connolly

Real-World Outcomes: Adapting Under Pressure

A finance team from a large regional bank was halfway through a culinary challenge when they realized their protein was missing. Instead of pausing, they swapped ingredients, changed the menu, and impressed the judges. Their facilitator said, That was the best metaphor for market agility I ve seen all year.

- ### 3. Collaborative Communication

Communication involves more than just talking. It includes listening, clarifying, sharing space, asking for help, delegating clearly, and giving and receiving feedback in real time.

In the kitchen, poor communication ruins food.

In the workplace, it destroys teams.

In today's digital age, texting has become one of the most overused and misunderstood forms of communication.

While it offers speed and convenience, it often falls short in effectiveness—especially in situations where clarity, nuance, and mutual understanding are crucial.

The main flaw of texting is that it functions as a **one-way form of communication**. It assumes everyone shares the same definitions, interpretations, and emotional contexts surrounding words. But they don't.

Language is deeply personal, shaped by individual experiences, culture, and emotion. When we rely solely on texting—or any one-sided form of communication—we risk misunderstandings, misinterpretations, and sometimes conflict.

Collaborative communication is different. It's not just "I talk, you listen."

It's about exploring together, clarifying, and co-creating understanding.

The goal of Collaborative Communication is to discover the truth rather than just exchanging information. It involves:

- Active listening
- Reflective feedback
- Emotional Intelligence
- A readiness to ask questions rather than make assumptions.

Misunderstandings occur when communication is rigid—when it relies on a single perspective, definition, or meaning.

It's presumptuous to assume that your interpretation is the only correct one. In a truly collaborative environment, **meaning is constructed together**, not dictated.

That's why effective communication must be **paired with collaboration**.

It's not enough to send a message; you need to build a bridge.

Effective communication during collaboration boosts trust, enhances alignment, and drives genuine innovation.

In business, as in life, connection isn't created by talking at people.

It's created by talking with them.

To highlight how important communication is, I want to share a story from my own life.

I've always enjoyed trying different ethnic foods, and Vietnamese cuisine holds a special place in my heart. Over time,

I set a personal goal to order my meals in their native language—not because I spoke it fluently, but to help bridge the cultural gap, even if just a little.

The first time I tried this language feat, the reaction was priceless.

The server looked at me with a confused expression, trying to understand my awkward pronunciation. But as I pointed to the menu item while doing my best to say the Vietnamese name, something magical happened.

The server's face lit up with a big smile. At that moment, they understood—not just what I was trying to order, but that I was **making an effort** to connect.

Sometimes, they would even call over a few other restaurant staff to listen to the "big American guy" do his best in their language.

What happened next was more than just laughter—it was *acceptance.*

Suddenly, I wasn't just another customer at the lunch counter. I felt like I bel*onged with them.*

The impact didn't end there. Every time I returned to that restaurant, they remembered me. They greeted me warmly, gave me the best seat, provided excellent service, and served the finest dishes the kitchen had.

All of this comes **from simply taking the time to communicate honestly.**

And here's the real lesson: It didn't matter that my Vietnamese wasn't perfect. It didn't matter that I stumbled over the words. **What mattered was that I tried.**

In communication, **effort matters.** Perfect technique isn't the main factor for connection—*intention* is.

When people see that you truly care enough to meet them halfway, barriers break down, relationships build, and real connection occurs.

In leadership, team-building, and life—effo**rt is what counts most.**

◆ 4. Action-Oriented Culture

There's no "maybe" in the kitchen. It's move or miss the moment.

TAC™ teaches teams to *act with purpose*—to organize, to execute, and to finish strong.

It's where the team understands: **"If we don't do this together, it won't get done at all."**

In a professional kitchen, there's no room for "maybe." There's no time for endless debate, second-guessing, or analysis paralysis.

You either **move with purpose**—or you **miss the moment**.

The environment demands intentional action.

- Handling tasks without waiting for perfect conditions
- Making confident decisions, even when under pressure
- Finish strong, because being halfway there isn't truly being done.

TAC™ promotes this vital mindset in teams. It motivates individuals to not wait for instructions but to **think proactively, take initiative, and share responsibility for the results**. It transforms groups from passive participants into active collaborators.

The realization hits quickly in the kitchen: 'If we don't do this together, it won't get done at all."

There isn't just one hero who saves the day.

Success is a team effort — or it's not truly success at all.

In business, the same idea applies. Teams that are trained to act decisively and work together become faster, smarter, and more adaptable. They fix problems before they get worse. They respond to market changes smoothly without chaos.

They beat competitors stuck in "maybe."

An action-oriented culture provides a competitive edge.
It's not about rushing recklessly; instead, it's about coordinated, committed effort toward a common goal.

Through TAC™, teams don't just talk about solutions.

They **embody** the solution—working together in real time and acting in unity.

- **5. Ownership and Accountability**

Cooking shows who is responsible for the outcome, who takes the lead, and who supports others without needing to be asked.

It's not about who leads; it's about who shows up and follows through.

TAC™ vs. Traditional Team Building: What's Changing?

Feature	Traditional Team Building	TAC™ – Team Associative Conditioning
Fun Factor	✓	✓
Sensory Engagement	✗	✓
Business Behavior Transfer	✗	✓
Trust + Communication Skills	✗	✓
Internal Accountability	✗	✓
Cultural Impact	✗	✓

This chapter introduces TAC™.

In the upcoming chapters, we'll demonstrate how it works in real-life situations—explaining why cooking is an ideal way to learn and how companies across various industries are using it to transform their culture from within.

So don't just train your team.

Condition them for excellence.

Takeaway Recipe

In this chapter, we introduce **TAC™—Team Associative Conditioning**—a sensory-driven framework that transforms traditional team building into a strategic cultural tool. Unlike typical events that entertain but rarely change behavior, TAC™ uses emotional and physical experiences to reinforce trust, adaptability, collaboration, action, and ownership. Whether under tight deadlines or in the heat of the moment, TAC™ helps teams operate with clarity, accountability, and cohesion. By engaging multiple senses and anchoring behaviors through real-time experiences, TAC™ sets the stage for lasting culture change, offering a repeatable, reliable way to turn moments into momentum.

Time to Stir It Up

1. Which of the five TAC™ pillars (trust, adaptability, communication, action, accountability) do you see as the most vital—or the most missing—in your current team culture?

2. Can you recall a time when a multisensory or emotionally intense moment, such as a major launch or a shared challenge, affected your team's performance or relationships?

3. How can hands-on experiences like cooking act as a leadership lab for your team—especially in high-pressure situations?

CHAPTER 4

WHY COOKING?

"One of the wonderful things about the restaurant business is that it attracts people from wildly diverse backgrounds and forces them to get along, to cooperate, to come to understand one another."

— *Anthony Bourdain*

Chapter Highlights

- Why cooking isn't just a metaphor for collaboration but a powerful, sensory strategy for leadership growth

- The difference between traditional "team building" and experiential transformation

- How The Corporate Culinary Challenge™ simulates real business dynamics in a kitchen environment

- Stories from actual events that show how cooking connects, reveals, and inspires

- The top key takeaways for leaders—and how those translate into business ROI

◆ **The Real Power of Culinary Team Building**

When people first hear "cooking team building," many imagine a laid-back activity with good food, laughter, and maybe some friendly competition. While those elements definitely are part of it, what makes the **Corporate Culinary Challenge**™ unique is what's beneath the surface: a carefully designed, sensory-based team learning experience that mirrors the real-world business environment.

Think of it as a pressure cooker made for a specific purpose.

Cooking requires teamwork, communication, decision-making under pressure, creative problem solving, and often—improvisation. What better environment to observe, coach, and strengthen a group's ability to function as a cohesive, high-performing team?

- **The Challenge Behind the Aprons**

Unlike typical cooking classes that focus on recipes and culinary techniques, the **Corporate Culinary Challenge**™ omits those elements. No recipes. No culinary training required. No pre-assigned roles. Teams arrive as professionals—such as finance managers, engineers, and healthcare leaders—and leave as communicators, collaborators, and coaches.

Each team gets a basket of multicultural ingredients, a common goal (to create a gourmet buffet in less than 90 minutes), and a leadership decision: who will serve as their **Chef de Cuisine**? This mirrors typical business conditions—tight deadlines, unclear initial structure, diverse team makeup, and the pressure to succeed.

As a facilitator, I design the program using the **TAC**™ **Process** (Team ® Action ® Culture), which is rooted in a scalable model of cultural transformation. Participants are not just learning to cook—they are experiencing what it feels like to build a culture of accountability, flexibility, and trust in real time.

◆ Three Layers of Learning

1. Team Dynamics Exposed

Team behavior under time pressure reveals a lot about individuals. Who takes initiative? Who works together naturally? Who pulls back? Who bonds the team? In the cooking challenge, teams expose unspoken dynamics that often remain hidden in everyday office life.

One team at a global consulting firm realized they had been isolated for years, rarely collaborating across divisions. But when they faced missing pieces and recognized they needed help from another team, they developed a communication liaison system entirely on their own. Later, a senior partner remarked, "We've talked about interdepartmental coordination for five years. We *did* it tonight in less than 90 minutes."

2. Leadership Under Pressure

When time is limited and information is incomplete, leadership naturally emerges. In some teams, the assigned Chef de Cuisine struggles to stay on course, while in others, informal leaders step up—those who ask the right questions, turn confusion into clarity, or calm nerves during chaos.

A memorable moment happened at a pharmaceutical company's offsite. A team lost its Chef midway through the challenge due to a planned facilitator switch—a simulation of what happens when leadership changes unexpectedly. At first, the team froze. Then, one participant who was previously quiet stepped forward. "Let's finish this together," she said. That team not only finished early but also won the challenge.

3. Culture in Action

Cooking side by side encourages team members to be themselves. Flour on their aprons, chopping boards to clean, and sauces to sample reveal their authentic selves. This environment fosters honest conversations, playful teasing, and pride in what they create together.

After one Corporate Culinary Challenge, a VP from a Fortune 500 tech company shared: "I saw sides of my people I've never seen—who they are when they're not behind titles. I'll lead differently starting Monday."

- **Why Cooking Works: A Sensory Science**

The magic of this experience isn't just emotional — it's neurological. Cooking stimulates multiple senses simultaneously. Sight, sound, touch, taste, and smell connect with the brain far more deeply than abstract conversation or slides ever could. As neuroscience confirms, **multi-sensory learning** enhances memory formation through **dopamine and oxytocin**, the brain chemicals linked to trust, satisfaction, and connection.

That's why we remember the smell of freshly baked bread or the exact taste of a childhood dish—much more vividly than a quarterly all-hands meeting.

By engaging the entire brain and body, cooking becomes a **transformative anchor**—a memory your team will not just remember but also reflect on as a turning point in how they collaborate and lead.

- **Customized, Strategic, and Results-Driven**

A key feature that makes our program unique is its **customization**. Before each event, we work with clients to clarify the desired outcomes—whether it involves strengthening interdepartmental relationships, onboarding a new leadership team, or increasing accountability.

Here's how we tailor the experience:

- **Scheduling meetings** with your HR or leadership sponsor

- **Conducting pre-event surveys** to evaluate team needs and dynamics

- **Incorporating learning moments** aligned with your culture and values

- **Leading debriefs** that transform experiences into business insights

- **Providing post-program summaries** to reinforce key takeaways and outline next steps

Our programs are available to organizations across different industries—from **tech and pharma** to **finance, healthcare, and higher education.**

◆ **Case Snapshot: OrgDynamics Consulting Group**

In June 2025, we partnered with **OrgDynamics Consulting Group** to host a customized Corporate Culinary Challenge® for their client's leadership retreat in Houston, Texas.

The Objective: Align 24 senior leaders, build trust, and improve communication.

The Challenge: Create a gourmet multicultural buffet without a recipe in just 90 minutes. **The Outcome**: All teams succeeded. The experience revealed hidden leaders, resolved long-standing interpersonal conflicts, and started a new tradition—monthly cross-departmental lunches at HQ.

◆ **Two Key Insights for Every Leader**

1. People remember what they experience, not what they're told.

You can teach collaboration—or create an environment where it's practiced, assessed, and celebrated. Cooking provides that environment.

2. Culture isn't created in conference rooms—it's made in moments.

Moments of challenge, laughter, feedback, and pride. When these moments are well-crafted, they resonate throughout your organization long after the event.

◆ What Sets It Apart?

Let's be honest: there's a lot of noise in the team-building industry. Escape rooms, ropes courses, wine tastings—all can be fun. But few activities combine effective facilitation, real results, multi-sensory participation, and strong metaphors for business.

The Corporate Culinary Challenge® does.

That's why we call it more than just a "cooking event." It's a leadership laboratory—disguised as dinner.

Takeaway Recipe

Chapter 4 illustrates how cooking serves as a powerful metaphor and practical approach for leadership and team transformation. We clarify the difference between a typical cooking class and our unique Culinary Challenge model—showing how it promotes collaboration, examines team dynamics, and produces measurable, memorable results. Aligned closely with your organizational goals and based on the TAC™ methodology, our cooking team building goes beyond just an activity. It marks the beginning of a new culture.

◊ Time to Stir It Up

1. When was the last time your team experienced a high-trust, low-risk setting to practice real collaboration?

2. What underlying dynamics are present in your team—and how could an experiential setting reveal them?

3. How can a sensory-based learning event like the Corporate Culinary Challenge® support your culture goals this year?

CHAPTER 5

CREATING THE ULTIMATE COOKING TEAM BUILDING EXPERIENCE

'The military taught me discipline, how to problem solve, teamwork, and loyalty, a perfect parallel to the kitchen."

— *Robert Irvine, Restaurant: Impossible*

Chapter Highlights

- Learn how to tailor your culinary team-building to achieve your company's main engagement and development goals.

- Identify the critical questions to ask before designing your experience.

- Explore methods to align outcomes with your team culture, leadership objectives, and business environment.

- Learn how logistics, group dynamics, and facilitation style influence the success of your session.

- Get a practical planning guide that can be used internally or with a provider like CEO Chef.

Creating the ideal Cooking Team Building program isn't just about the food — it's about establishing the right **atmosphere,**

purpose, and results. Whether you're part of a Fortune 500 executive team or a fast-growing startup, your team deserves an experience as intentional as your business strategy.

Step 1: Clarify the main goal of the event

Begin by asking before selecting menus, locations, or dates.

- What results are we expecting from this event?
    - Building relationships?
    - Leadership training?
    - Cross-department collaboration?
    - Celebration and morale boost?

This will determine whether your session has a casual or impactful tone. For example, if your goal is to align hybrid teams, you might include structured activities during the meal to simulate real-life collaboration challenges.

Step 2: Know Your Audience

Is your group mainly analytical, creative, competitive, or a combination of these? Knowing your participants helps tailor the culinary experience.

- Analytical groups tend to respond well to **problem-solving methods**.
- Creatives appreciate **fusion menus** and versatile plating styles.
- Sales teams may enjoy a competitive cooking contest.
- HR or executive teams might favor **introspective, leadership-oriented formats**.

Adjust your programming style to align with the team's personality.

Step 3: Match the Format to Your Schedule and Space

Your event could happen:

- In a hotel conference room, corporate kitchen, or an outside venue.
- Whether indoors or outdoors, with or without access to a kitchen.
- During a 90-minute session or an entire day retreat.

What matters most is the **flow**, not the setting. Think about whether your team would benefit more from a quick burst of fun or an all-day activity that strengthens team resilience.

Step 4: Choose a Menu That Aligns with Your Message

The food should not only taste good but also serve as a metaphor.

Examples:

- **International Buffet** ® Showcases diversity and global teamwork.
- **Farm-to-Table:** Represents sustainability, health, or transparency.
- **Iron Chef Format** ® Emphasizes innovation and leadership under pressure.

A themed menu reinforces your values and enhances the experience's memorability.

Step 5: Use a Facilitated Debrief to Reinforce Learning

Don't stop after the last bite. A facilitated debrief links the lessons learned in the kitchen to real-world situations in the boardroom.

- Who rose to the challenge under pressure?
- What breakdowns occurred and how were they fixed?
- Where did collaboration and communication stand out?

This is the special moment when the team sees themselves differently—and so do their leaders.

Step 6: Add Takeaway Tools and Follow-Up

If your team's experience stops at dessert, you've missed the best chance to boost ROI.

Enhance the learning with:

- A summary of group dynamics following the event
- Cooking Lessons for Business Worksheet
- Leader-specific feedback tools
- A brief follow-up coaching session or digital recap.

Sample Experience Design:

Client Objective: Promote cross-functional collaboration among sales, operations, and marketing.

Design Solution:

- Theme: Ultimate Cooking Championship®
- Teams were merged across departments.
- Hidden ingredients are added midstream to simulate real-time disruptions.
- The debrief emphasized agility, communication, and adaptability. **Outcome:** The team reported increased empathy and better cross-team communication after the event, resulting in a 22% reduction in project delivery errors over the following quarter.

Takeaway Recipe

A cooking team-building experience is only as effective as its design. The best ones are intentional, strategic, and aligned with your business goals. By focusing on the **who, why, what**, and **how**, you create a transformative program that nurtures not just the team but also the company culture. From custom themes to tailored debriefs, this approach turns a fun day into a major growth milestone.

◐ Time to Stir It Up

1. What is the biggest challenge your team is currently facing, and how might a culinary simulation demonstrate that challenge?

2. What team behaviors or leadership qualities do you want to see and develop in a kitchen setting?

3. How can this experience act as both a bonding opportunity and a strategic benefit for your business?

CHAPTER 6

THE HIDDEN HEAT BEHIND HIGH-PERFORMANCE TEAMS

"People will forget what you said, people will forget what you did, but people will never forget how you made them feel."

— *Maya Angelou*

Chapter Highlights

- Discover why emotional intelligence and intentional respect form the basis of high-performing teams.

- Learn how small acts of recognition can build strong loyalty and boost morale.

- Explore why attention—authentic, focused presence—is one of the most powerful leadership tools today.

- Learn how warmth, kindness, and understanding enhance both internal team dynamics and external vendor relationships.

- See how companies like Chewy build lasting brand loyalty through emotional connection, and what that means for your organization.

Every successful kitchen knows that flavor is about more than just ingredients—it's about chemistry. The same applies to high-performing teams. Whether you're in a boardroom or on a busy kitchen line, the quality of your relationships affects the results you achieve. In this chapter, we explore the subtle art of building professional, respectful, and collaborative relationships with colleagues, partners, and vendors—a philosophy based on mutual respect, acknowledgment, attentiveness, and presence.

The Foundation: Professional Respect

Respect in a professional setting isn't just about holding a title; it's demonstrated and reciprocated through everyday actions. From your tone of voice to how you greet a coworker or respond to a vendor, respect serves as an unspoken agreement that fosters teamwork.

In the culinary world, chefs understand that neglecting your prep team, ingredients, or timing can cause the dish to fall apart. Similarly, showing respect in the office—by arriving on time, listening attentively, and valuing each person's role—helps build a culture of trust. Teams thrive when mutual respect exists, and performance naturally improves.

The Power of Acknowledgment

In most work environments, acknowledgment is often undervalued. However, it has the power to change dynamics instantly. Taking a moment to thank a teammate for their input or to recognize a vendor's effort to meet a deadline sets a positive tone. Acknowledgment doesn't need grand gestures; it's as simple as a verbal thank you, a handwritten note, or publicly praising someone's contribution during a meeting.

People want to feel recognized. When team members and partners see that their contributions are acknowledged, their commitment to the shared mission strengthens. Recognition isn't just about boosting egos; it's about building human connections—the kind that fosters loyalty, improves morale, and raises standards for everyone.

Attention Is the Ultimate Currency

In today's distracted world, one of the most valuable gifts you can give someone is your complete, undivided attention. When you speak with a colleague, turning off your phone, making eye contact, and truly listening demonstrate leadership.

Being present is a skill, and when practiced deliberately, it becomes the foundation of effective communication. Whether you're negotiating with a vendor, mentoring a new employee, or strategizing with a colleague, the ability to be fully in the moment builds trust. And where trust exists, progress follows.

The Unspoken Ingredient: Professional Warmth

Although we don't call it "affection" in corporate language, every strong professional relationship has a layer of warmth. It's evident in the sincerity of your tone, the encouragement in your words, and the small yet meaningful gestures—like bringing an extra coffee to a coworker on a busy morning.

Professional warmth builds connections. It reminds team members that they matter beyond their roles. Just as a seasoned chef knows when to add a hint of spice to enhance a dish, a workplace leader must recognize when to blend professionalism with empathy. When colleagues feel cared for—not coddled, but respected and appreciated—they are more motivated to do their best.

Vendor Relationships: Seeing Partners as Allies, Not Just Transactions

Vendors are often the most overlooked relationships in the corporate ecosystem. However, just like the purveyors of fine ingredients in a kitchen, they are essential to your success. Treating vendors as partners rather than just suppliers improves the entire operation.

Building long-term vendor relationships based on consistency, communication, and shared goals encourages alignment. Return calls promptly and clearly state expectations. When vendors exceed expectations, recognize their efforts. These small gestures build loyalty and trust, turning a single transaction into a reliable partnership.

Colleagues and Associates: The Internal Network

Within every business, a network of relationships exists that, when nurtured, becomes a source of innovation, support, and momentum. Colleagues are not just people you pass in the hallway or include in an email; they are your internal partners.

Great leaders know how to unify departments, respect different communication styles, and foster synergy among personalities. They accomplish this through transparency, integrity, and emotional intelligence. By encouraging open dialogue, breaking down silos, and building a shared purpose, collaboration becomes smooth and effective.

Creating the Environment: Culture by Design™

Culture isn't left to chance; it's cultivated. Similar to a kitchen's mise en place, your corporate environment should be intentional and thoughtful. This involves building a culture where respect, acknowledgment, attention, and warmth are practiced daily, not just talked about during HR trainings.

Start meetings with a quick highlight of someone's achievement. Encourage managers to give "micro shoutouts." Dedicate time for celebrating humanity, birthdays, milestones, and personal successes. These micro-cultures nurture the core of retention, productivity, and pride.

Emotional Intelligence as a Business Strategy

Building relationships isn't just about soft skills; it's strategic. Emotional intelligence in leadership has become a key predictor of team performance and business success. Empathy, self-awareness, and interpersonal skills are now essential, not optional.

A company that values strong internal and external relationships moves faster, communicates more effectively, and retains talent longer. The ripple effect of emotionally intelligent leadership impacts everything, from customer experience to profitability.

❋ If you are unfamiliar with **Chewy**, you probably don't own a cat or dog. They offer a great selection of supplies, food, beds, and other items, including pet pharmaceuticals.

The customer journey with Chewy is more than effortless; it's genuinely enjoyable to work with them. What sets them apart from similar companies is that they show genuine care.

One particular time, they caught our pups being held in our arms. They took virtual screenshots of our pups and asked for their names to share with the office. Later that month, we received four blocks of wood, each measuring six by six inches, with our pup's image burned into the wood. That thoughtful gesture touched our hearts, and that day solidified Chewy as our pet provider for life!

How would you like others to see you as a lifelong supplier or vendor in your industry?

Just as a great meal is remembered for the feelings it evokes, so too are a great leader, a great team, and a great business. Relationships are the true recipe for lasting success. When colleagues feel respected, acknowledged, and genuinely supported, they perform not out of obligation but out of inspiration.

When vendors are seen as collaborators, the ecosystem operates more smoothly, intelligently, and with greater integrity. This chapter encourages you to approach your leadership style with the same intention and care that you put into your cooking. Ultimately, business isn't just about the bottom line; it's about the people who help you build it.

Takeaway Recipe

In this chapter, we've examined the true value of workplace excellence—relationships. Just like preparing a five-star dish, building high-performing teams requires careful ingredients: mutual respect, consistent recognition, meaningful attention, and genuine warmth. These qualities are tangible—they can be observed, repeated, and are strategically essential for both internal collaboration and external partnerships. By adopting this human-centered approach, leaders and organizations cultivate cultures that retain talent, increase engagement, and promote sustainable success. Just as a chef knows that flavor depends on more than ingredients, visionary leaders understand that performance relies on more than just skill—it depends on connection.

Time to Stir It Up

1. What small but consistent actions can you take to demonstrate respect and appreciation to your team and partners this week?

2. Reflect on a moment when you felt genuinely recognized and valued at work. What made that experience special, and how can you help someone else feel the same way?

3. How could treating your vendors or suppliers as genuine allies improve results in your daily operations?

CHAPTER 7

THE MECHANICS OF CONNECTION

"Relationships don't just make work more enjoyable. They make work work. And when organizations design for connection, they don't just retain people. They unleash them."

— *Dr. Renee Gordon*

Chapter Highlights

- Discover why relationships are not only emotional soft skills but also essential strategic elements that influence organizational performance.

- Explore the **three levels of relational leadership** (Top-Down, Peer-to-Peer, Outside-In) and see how each fosters trust and alignment both within and outside the organization.

- Identify simple, repeatable **daily habits** that foster relational equity and enhance team cohesion in high-pressure environments.

- Be inspired by real-life examples—from companies like Chewy to everyday "extra plate" moments—that show how small relational efforts can create big cultural changes.

- Learn how to **transform connections into systems** with the TAC™ framework and Culture by Design™ to create a sustainable, high-trust workplace.

How to Build and Maintain Relationships That Drive Performance

Strong relationships are the core of every successful organization. As mentioned in the previous chapter, relationships are not just soft skills—they serve as a strategic asset. They affect how information moves, how teams react under pressure, and how deeply people connect with each other and with the mission.

However, recognizing the importance of relationships isn't enough.

To truly harness their power, you must actively cultivate them.

This chapter details specific, repeatable actions that enhance relational equity within your culture, based on our TAC™ model (Team Associative Conditioning).

♦ 1. Build from the Center Out: Three Levels of Relationship Strategy

Every organization has three relational layers. Recognizing and nurturing each one is crucial.

▸ Top-Down (Leaders to Teams)

Leadership should model consistency and emotional availability. Replace performance-only check-ins with pulse conversations. Don't just discuss outcomes—ask, "How are you doing?" Use micro-recognitions: handwritten notes, thoughtful affirmations, and verbal acknowledgments that show employees they are seen and valued.

*TAC™ **Practice:*** In team cooking experiences, leaders join their staff in the kitchen—not just to observe, but to participate.

Cooking shoulder-to-shoulder dissolves hierarchy and highlights shared humanity.

▸ Peer-to-Peer (Teammates Supporting Each Other)

Authentic collaboration thrives when individuals see they're not competing but contributing. Introduce rituals like "Shout-Out Fridays," where team members celebrate each other's successes. Try "Role Swap Days" to build empathy—such as an engineer helping marketing or sales shadowing customer service.

TAC™ Practice: Cooking together relies on interdependence. One person prepares, another plates, and someone else cleans—no one succeeds unless everyone is in sync. It's contribution, not credit, that drives progress.

▸ Outside-In (Vendors, Clients, Stakeholders)

Relational excellence extends beyond your company's boundaries. Build partnerships based on shared values rather than just transactional needs. Take time to celebrate successes with your clients. Arrange "just because" check-ins—not to sell, but to connect.

TAC™ Practice: We invite clients to participate actively—not as spectators, but as co-creators. Sharing a meal together is not just a metaphor; it's literal. Relationships formed over shared meals tend to endure.

♦ 2. Daily Habits That Build Relational Equity

Don't wait for team-building retreats or formal evaluations. Real connections are built daily—in hallway conversations, mid-project frustrations, and spontaneous moments of kindness.

Simple Daily Habits:

- Ask: "What color is your energy today—Green, Yellow, or Red?" Then, take a moment to truly listen.

- End each meeting with a positive thank you.
- Celebrate small victories: a thoughtful email, a creative solution, a kind gesture.

Leadership Reminder: Predictability fosters trust. When people see you are consistent in your care and concern, they respond more genuinely and perform with more confidence.

◆ 3. Case Stories: The Ripple Effect of a Relationship-Focused Culture

Case Study: Chewy—The Company That Cares

In today's highly automated, bottom-line-focused corporate culture, genuine connection is a rare find. However, there are shining examples that show connection doesn't become *easier with* growth—it actually grows *because* of care.

Chewy, an online pet supply retailer, is one such example.

Over time, we built a relationship with Chewy—not through a sales rep or a fancy program, but through heartfelt gestures. At home, we care for five joyful dogs, 47 exotic parrots, and five aquariums, the largest being 350 gallons. This means constant pet care—filters, food, vitamins, and toys. We order from Chewy regularly.

One day, a package arrived unexpectedly. Inside was a hand-painted portrait of our three little Maltese girl pups—each lovingly adorned with bows and colorful dresses. Weeks later, we received another portrait—this time of one of our favorite parrots, painted with vibrant detail. These weren't mass-produced gifts. Someone on their team had taken the time to look through our photos, understand our pets 'personalities, and create something truly meaningful.

When one of our beloved pets died, we got a condolence card. It wasn't just automatic; it was personal.

This is what happens when a company sees customers as relationships, not just revenue. Over the next four months, I shared that story with 67 people—friends, clients, neighbors, and strangers. I didn't mean to promote Chewy. I was simply moved, and when people are moved, they share.

Relational marketing isn't just about data—it's about creating joy. It's the ripple effect of intentional care.

Case Story: The Ministry of the Extra Plate

Connections aren't always made in boardrooms. Sometimes, they begin with an extra helping of food.

Over the years, in every city and neighborhood I've lived in—from Los Angeles to Chattanooga—I've practiced what I call "The Ministry of the Extra Plate." When I cook, I make a little extra. I package it up and quietly deliver it to someone who might be alone, busy, or simply weary.

Some neighbors are widowed. Some are single professionals who don't cook. Others are simply people going through tough times. I don't bring food because I pity them—I bring it because I respect them. I want them to feel seen. Valued. Remembered.

And then, during holidays—Easter, Thanksgiving, Christmas—I open my home to what I affectionately call the "holiday orphans." They aren't truly orphaned, of course. They're friends, neighbors, or acquaintances whose families live far away or whose life circumstances leave them alone on days meant for togetherness.

At our holiday table, there's always room for one more. We set the table beautifully, serve dishes made with love, and share stories that linger long after dessert.

There is no agenda, only presence.

This same spirit of generosity can be applied to the workplace. Imagine the results if leaders brought this level of care to the office—remembering birthdays, noticing a colleague's tired look, and offering help without being asked. The impact isn't just emotional; it's cultural.

A healthy workplace doesn't need to be perfect. It just needs to show humanity.

When your culture reflects "I see you, and you matter," loyalty strengthens, engagement increases, and excellence naturally follows when love is in action.

♦ 4. Building a Relationship-Driven Culture

If you want relationships to last, you need to make them a part of your core system.

We call this *Culture by Design*™—a philosophy that ensures relationship-building isn't random or reliant on individual personalities. It's consistent, predictable, and lasting.

Systems to Sustain:

- Integrate relational expectations into onboarding programs.
- Launch monthly "Team Connection Labs" featuring short relational exercises.
- Create tools for peer recognition: gratitude walls, shout-out channels, and culture coins.

TAC*™ *Connection: We often begin with a cooking session that helps break the ice, followed by structured reinforcement to sustain the relational habits. This experience is just the start; repetition is what builds culture.

♦ 5. Relationship Toolkit

- **Check-In Questions for Leaders:** How are you really doing? What excites you right now? What's one small win from this week?

- **Team Appreciation Prompts:** Name someone who helped you this week. What did they do? Why was it important?
- **Peer-to-Peer Conversation Starters:** What's something outside of work that makes you happy?
- **Personal Style Mapping Tool:** Discover communication styles and relationship drivers.
- **Feedback Script Templates:** Share your thoughts with respect and clarity.

These aren't just tools; they are relationship boosters.

Let us remember: Excellence doesn't start with systems. It begins in hearts.

Culture is what we build when we care—when we go beyond roles and titles and speak to the human behind the badge.

Whether you're leading a Fortune 500 company or managing a small local business, the principle stays the same: people matter. Valued people contribute more, stay longer, and become stronger.

That's the true power of a culture built on connection.

Takeaway Recipe

In this chapter, we transitioned from theory to practice by examining how relationships are built at every level of a modern organization. Using the TAC™ model, we learned that intentionality—not luck—drives lasting human connection. Through daily rituals, emotional pulse checks, and shared activities like cooking side-by-side, leaders and teams can foster trust that leads to greater engagement, resilience, and performance.

The most respected companies aren't necessarily the most polished—they're the most human. They focus on care rather than convenience, consistency rather than charisma, and presence rather than pretense. Whether through a heartfelt customer gesture or an extra plate shared at home, connection serves as the catalyst that turns culture from a concept into a competitive advantage.

If you want a culture where people go above and beyond, make sure they feel seen, valued, and connected. Building relationships isn't an extra; it's the glue that keeps excellence together.

🔥 Time to Stir It Up

1. Which of the three relationship levels—Top-Down, Peer-to-Peer, or Outside-In—seems the most underdeveloped in your organization? Why?

2. What is one daily habit you could begin tomorrow to build more relational equity with your team or clients?

3. How could your company culture change if every leader exemplified the kind of presence and care described in this chapter?

CHAPTER 8

THE NEUROSCIENCE OF FLAVOR AND PERFORMANCE

'The best executives understand that performance isn't just logical—it's emotional and sensory. If you want transformation, don't just teach. Create experience."

— Dr. Paul Zak, Neuroeconomist and author of Trust Factor

Chapter Highlights

- What if your team could **retain more, build trust more quickly, and perform better**—all by cooking together?

- Why does a single shared meal often foster a more lasting connection than a full-day workshop?

- Could the **ingredient lacking** in your leadership development strategy be *flavor*?

- What if your next training session stimulated dopamine, oxytocin—and yielded measurable results?

Why Cooking Triggers Culture

In a world where organizations are desperate for deeper engagement, faster innovation, and stronger collaboration, there's one sensory domain that corporate training has largely ignored—until now. Welcome to the intersection of neuroscience, food, and high performance.

This chapter explores the unexpected yet scientifically grounded connection between cooking and culture—and why engaging the senses through culinary experiences doesn't just feed your team's appetite but rewires their behavior.

Your Brain on Flavor: The Hidden Power of the Senses

When your brain encounters a stimulus—like the sizzle of garlic in a hot pan or the smell of fresh rosemary—something remarkable happens. Dopamine, the neurotransmitter responsible for pleasure and motivation, spikes. At the same time, oxytocin, the "bonding hormone," begins to circulate, enhancing feelings of trust and social connection.

These two neurochemicals—dopamine and oxytocin—form the biochemical foundation of all successful team-building. And they happen to be released naturally through cooking.

Why? Because food preparation is a multi-sensory experience. It activates every channel of perception:

- **Sight:** Colorful ingredients, vibrant plating, and movement
- **Sound:** Sizzling, chopping, the rhythm of teamwork
- **Touch:** Texture of dough, heat from the stove, tools in hand
- **Smell:** The most potent memory trigger in the human brain
- **Taste:** The ultimate shared reward and feedback loop

Traditional corporate training hits maybe one of these senses—usually sight (PowerPoint) or sound (lectures). But science tells us that we retain only about 10% of what we hear and 20% of what we read. Compare that to 80% retention when learning is both emotional and physical.

Cooking team building, especially when structured through TAC™ (Team Associative Conditioning), is a masterclass in emotional learning. It imprints behavior not just through repetition but through *association*—the neurological principle that ties memory to sensory context.

Why Do We Remember Grandma's Kitchen and Not Last Quarter's Strategy Deck?

Smell is directly linked to the limbic system—the part of the brain that processes memory and emotion. Unlike other senses, olfactory input bypasses the thalamus (the brain's switchboard) and goes straight to the amygdala and hippocampus.

This is why a single scent can transport you back decades. It's also why a cooking experience can embed team values— collaboration, ownership, creativity—far more effectively than a motivational keynote.

This isn't theoretical. It's neuroscience.

In fact, studies show that the **emotional salience** of an event is what drives long-term retention. When you feel something strongly—joy, urgency, pride—it becomes etched into your neural pathways.

That's what happens in a cooking team building program. Participants aren't just learning how to work together—they're *feeling* it. The rush of plating a dish under pressure. The camaraderie of shared tasks. The satisfaction of presenting a finished product to peers. These moments forge a memory far more powerful than any annual report ever could.

The Social Science of Food: Why We Bond When We Cook

Humans have been breaking bread together for millennia. In every culture, cuisine and connection are intertwined. Preparing and sharing food is one of the oldest forms of community building.

But why?

Because when people cook and eat together, they're engaged in a **shared ritual**—one that requires trust, coordination, and vulnerability. These are the same ingredients that define high-performing teams.

Research in organizational behavior shows that teams with high psychological safety—where members feel safe to take risks, admit mistakes, and express themselves—outperform their peers by nearly every metric.

Cooking naturally cultivates psychological safety. It disarms hierarchy (the CEO chops onions next to the intern), fosters spontaneous communication, and rewards experimentation.

One global healthcare client described it perfectly: "When we're in the kitchen, titles fall away. We're just people solving problems—together."

That's not just symbolic. It's systemic.

From Neuroplasticity to Team Dynamics

Neuroplasticity is the brain's ability to form new pathways through repeated experience. When you condition your team through multisensory, emotionally engaging activities—like a high-pressure cooking challenge—you're literally rewiring how they respond to stress, feedback, and collaboration.

Take this real-world example:

A multinational tech company integrated Cooking Team Building 2.0 into their leadership onboarding program. After one session, their HR director reported a measurable 27% increase in collaboration metrics (using pulse survey data). Why? Because the sensory and emotional anchoring made the lessons stick.

And here's the kicker: they remembered those insights *six months later*—not because they took notes, but because their bodies remembered the experience.

The Performance Loop: How Flavor Enhances Focus

The "performance loop" in team dynamics consists of four stages:

1. **Tension** – A challenge arises (e.g., a missing ingredient)
2. **Engagement** – Team members collaborate under pressure
3. **Resolution** – A solution is executed (the dish comes together)
4. **Reward** – The team experiences success (taste, praise, applause)

Cooking engages this loop faster and more vividly than almost any business scenario. And because the loop ends with *taste*, a primary sensory reward, the satisfaction is immediate and memorable.

That's a big deal in training. Most corporate programs delay rewards—sometimes indefinitely. But humans are wired for instant feedback. Flavor delivers that. And when teams associate that feedback with behaviors like trust, initiative, and adaptability, they begin to link *those behaviors* with success.

Sensory Anchors and Organizational Culture

At the cultural level, these sensory "anchors" begin to influence language, rituals, and shared stories.

For instance, a major financial firm now uses phrases like "Who's plating this project?" or "Let's not burn the sauce"—light-hearted, food-based metaphors that actually shape how they frame leadership and accountability.

More than metaphors, these anchors become internal symbols—emotional shorthand for behavior under pressure.

Over time, they condition the team's instincts.

Just like muscle memory helps a chef plate without thinking, *cultural memory* helps a team act in alignment without pausing for permission.

Practical Applications: What Executives Can Do

Want to hardwire your culture into your people? Start by engaging their senses and emotions.

Here's how elite organizations are leveraging the neuroscience of flavor and performance:

- **Sensory Immersion Workshops** – Using food to introduce new team values in a memorable way.
- **Leadership Simulations** – Culinary team-building sessions where execs role-play crisis scenarios and learn emotional agility.
- **Trust Rebuilding** – Cross-functional cooking experiences where silos are intentionally disrupted to restore communication.

Executives who model vulnerability in the kitchen—by asking for help, trying a new skill, or admitting they don't know something—send a powerful message: **We are all learners here.**

This flattens hierarchy and increases trust far more effectively than slogans ever could.

Why Cooking Triggers Culture

Culture isn't what's written on the wall—it's what happens under pressure.

It's who speaks up, who steps back, and how the team recalibrates when things go wrong.

Cooking team building, anchored in neuroscience, creates **miniature laboratories** for this behavior. Each session becomes a live-fire test of emotional regulation, communication, leadership, and execution.

Here's the magic: The memories created during those 90 minutes stick with your team—not just in their minds, but in their bodies.

And when the smells, sounds, and tastes of that experience reappear—say, at the office potluck or even a dinner at home—they trigger not just nostalgia, but a renewed sense of possibility.

They remember what it *felt* like to trust, to lead, to belong.

And that's what reshapes culture—not policies, but powerful, shared, sensory-anchored experiences.

Takeaway Recipe

In a world that often separates business from biology, this chapter reveals a crucial truth: your brain, your senses, and your team's performance are deeply connected.

Cooking activates all human senses—sight, sound, touch, smell, and taste—and stimulates the neurochemical systems responsible for trust, collaboration, and motivation. Dopamine encourages engagement. Oxytocin fosters connection. Additionally, flavor—more than just decoration—acts as a feedback mechanism that reinforces learning through reward.

This isn't just theoretical. Cooking team-building programs designed with TAC™ (Team Associative Conditioning) serve as immersive learning environments that promote lasting behavior change. From fostering psychological safety to reshaping cultural language and enhancing neuroplasticity, these culinary experiences build strong mental and emotional foundations.

At the organizational level, they offer a scalable, high-impact training approach. At the individual level, they promote a sense of belonging and reinforce behavioral memory—long after the aprons come off.

This is why cooking not only energizes your team but also transforms your culture from the inside out.

🍳 Time to Stir It Up

1. **Reflect** on the last training program your team completed. How much of it do you still remember three months later? Now, imagine that program had engaged all five senses—what might have been different?

2. What are some common rituals or symbols in your company culture today? Can sensory experiences like food, scent, or sound strengthen those shared identities?

3. Where do you see a need for increased psychological safety in your team? How might a collaborative cooking session act as a catalyst for building trust and encouraging open communication?

4. What leadership behaviors would you like to see more naturally demonstrated in your organization? Could those behaviors be improved through experiential learning rather than verbal instruction?

5. If you could redesign a key part of your team's culture using cooking as a metaphor or experience, what would it be—and what would success look (or taste) like?

CHAPTER 9

THE FUTURE OF WORK — WHY TAC™ IS THE CULTURAL MODEL OF THE 2030S

'The illiterate of the 21st century will not be those who cannot read and write, but those who cannot learn, unlearn, and relearn."

— Alvin Toffler

Chapter Highlights

- The workplace is undergoing rapid transformation—hybrid teams, cross-generational dynamics, and decentralized leadership are no longer future concepts; they are now daily realities.

- Traditional "culture-building" tactics—such as top-down communication, performance metrics, and one-off engagement initiatives—are losing relevance.

- This chapter introduces TAC™ (Team Associative Conditioning) as a powerful, neuroscience-backed framework that builds trust, agility, and emotional safety in real time.

- Drawing on research from McKinsey and Deloitte, we'll explore why emotional intelligence, sensory learning, and behavioral conditioning are the cornerstones of thriving future teams.

- A side-by-side scenario reveals how TAC™-trained teams outperform disconnected ones—offering a compelling look at how culture becomes your greatest strategic advantage.

Why the Future Requires a New Operating System

The workplace of 2030 is not just around the corner—it's already in your conference room, your Zoom windows, and your exit interviews. The old models of culture—built on hierarchy, isolated departments, and outdated training modules—are being outpaced by a workforce that demands agility, trust, inclusion, and meaning.

We now know what research confirms: the highest-performing companies of tomorrow will not be those with the largest budgets, but rather those that cultivate the strongest connections.

So what does that look like?

Welcome to TAC™: Team Associative Conditioning—a behavior-shaping, emotionally intelligent, multisensory cultural framework designed for the next decade of leadership.

The Emergence of Non-Negotiables

According to McKinsey, emotional intelligence, adaptability, and collaboration will be the most crucial skills for the next 5–10 years. Deloitte's Human Capital Trends report emphasizes the necessity for decentralized leadership, human-centered design, and learning cultures integrated into the workflow, not added on top of it.

It's no longer solely about what your team knows; it's about how they interact, how they adapt under pressure, and whether they trust each other to deliver without micromanagement.

That's why the future of work must prioritize:

- **Neuroscience-based learning (not just knowledge download)**
- **Peer-to-peer leadership** instead of top-down authority
- **Emotional and sensory memory anchoring** (beyond spreadsheets and slide decks)
- **Shared identity and psychological safety, rather** than solely focusing on performance metrics.

TAC™ as a Future-Ready Operating System

TAC™ isn't just a program; it's an *operating system*—one that seamlessly integrates into the behaviors, mindsets, and rituals defining your culture.

Let's compare:

Culture Challenge	Traditional Solution	TAC™ Solution
Hybrid disconnection	More Zoom check-ins	Shared sensory experiences (like cooking) to create anchor moments
Leadership pipeline gaps	Formal succession planning	BE-DO-HAVE model training via immersive practice
Turnover and disengagement	Engagement surveys	Real-time bonding through trust-based team pressure
Silos between departments	All-hands meetings	Cross-functional culinary simulations requiring mutual dependence

TAC™ teaches individuals to *experience* trust, collaborate effectively, and *develop* leadership skills by conditioning them in real-time, with real stakes.

Generational Alignment Through Common Understanding

By 2030, five generations will work side by side. From Gen Z's desire for purpose to Boomers 'need for recognition, each generation has slightly different needs.

What do they all have in common?

The desire to be significant.

TAC™ transcends generational preferences by providing:

- **Immersive shared challenges** that transcend age and hierarchy
- **Hands-on opportunities for contribution** (where everyone plays a vital role)
- **Personal visibility** (through group dynamics and reflection)
- **Built-in mentorship opportunities** (as experienced teammates assist newer ones in thriving)

In a world where most employees crave belonging, TAC™ creates teams that don't just tolerate each other—they trust, challenge, and *choose* one another.

A Real-Time Comparison: TAC™-Trained Team vs. Disconnected Team

Imagine this:

Scenario: Your hybrid marketing and sales teams are launching a major product under tight deadlines. Leadership is primarily remote. The pressure is intense.

Without TAC™ Training:

- Zoom fatigue sets in.
- Sales blames Marketing for delays.
- Internal chat turns passive-aggressive.
- Turnover risk increases as stress escalates.
- Leadership rushes to "restore morale."

With TAC™ Trained Team:

- Team members utilize a common emotional vocabulary acquired during the TAC™ event.
- Cross-functional ownership is anticipated and demonstrated.
- A sales rep jumps in to finish a marketing script—because that's how they worked in the kitchen.
- Weekly micro-coaching strengthens behavior modeling.
- The team finishes ahead of the deadline—*together*.

TAC™ Is Not a Trend—It's a Transformation

By 2030, leading companies won't set themselves apart by what they sell, but by how their teams function.

They will win through:

- Creating cultures that develop in real time.
- Training involves not only knowledge but also *behavior under pressure*.
- Developing *identity-driven* leadership rather than authority based on roles.
- Treat psychological safety as a baseline, not a bonus.

TAC™ doesn't replace your staff—it enhances their operating system.

Final Thought: Don't Prepare for the Future—Create It

If you're a VP, CHRO, or executive sponsor aiming to enhance your culture, retain your top performers, and lead the next generation, this isn't optional.

This represents your advantage.

Teams that excel in uncertainty aren't lucky—they're conditioned.

Let's refrain from reacting to change.

Let's begin *training for it.*

Welcome to TAC™—the future of culture, now available.

Takeaway Recipe

As the workforce evolves into a blend of remote, hybrid, and cross-generational collaboration, traditional leadership models and cultural strategies are becoming obsolete. The future isn't about more software, meetings, or rules—it's about deeper connections, agile behaviors, and emotional resonance.

In this forward-looking chapter, we examine how the demands of the 2030 workplace redefine what it means to lead, collaborate, and grow a resilient team culture. As work becomes more distributed and multigenerational, companies must replace outdated practices with immersive, emotionally intelligent systems that condition how teams behave, not just what they know.

Team Associative Conditioning (TAC™) provides a forward-facing operating system for culture—one that aligns neuroscience, behavioral design, and immersive team experiences to hardwire the habits and trust your team needs to thrive. Supported by insights from McKinsey, Deloitte, and real-world applications, TAC™ enhances team performance through experience, not theory.

Instead of merely reacting to change, TAC™-driven cultures take the initiative to design it—making them not only prepared for the future but also accountable for shaping it.

The future of work is already here, and TAC™ is your way to prepare for it.

◆ Time to Stir It Up

1. Which of the future-ready competencies outlined in this chapter—emotional intelligence, peer-to-peer leadership, sensory anchoring, or psychological safety—does your organization need to develop most urgently?

2. How well-equipped is your team to navigate ambiguity and perform under pressure? What experiences (if any) currently simulate those conditions safely?

3. In what ways could you begin integrating TAC™ practices into your leadership development or onboarding programs this year?

4. What does a "culture operating system" look like in your organization today—and how might it need to evolve by 2030?

CHAPTER 10

CREATING LEADERS TO BUILD TEAMS: BECOMING THE LEADER YOU'RE MEANT TO BE

"The real paycheck people cash every day isn't on paper—it's the feeling that what they do matters."

— *Jim Connolly, CEO Chef*

Chapter Highlights

- Explore how leadership begins with *who you choose to BE—*ing before titles, tasks, or results follow.

- Discover the BE → DO → HAVE framework that helps individuals embody leadership at every level of your organization.

- Discover how peer-to-peer leadership boosts collaboration, performance, and innovation through six key traits.

- See how switching from "expert" to "coach" changes not just results—but also culture.

- Explore real-life stories from the kitchen that show how distributed leadership fosters collective success.

Great teams don't form by accident—they are built through intentional leadership, purpose-driven actions, and a mindset of BE-ing before DO-ing. This chapter examines the transformational power of peer-to-peer leadership, how to cultivate leadership from within, and why developing leaders at every level boosts the performance and culture of your organization.

The Power of Purpose-Driven Leadership

During my years as the chef-owner of a high-end French/Swiss restaurant, I discovered that kitchen leadership depends less on hierarchy and more on mindset. One key leadership tool I used was an exercise in forward identity: asking each team member not only where they saw themselves in five years, but also who they would need to BE today to reach that goal.

I'd like to share a story.

One of my younger cooks, full of passion but still inexperienced, shared that his dream was to become a certified executive pastry chef, maybe even run his own patisserie. I told him, "If you commit yourself to learning and growing for the next two years, I'll help you get there. But in return, you must start BE-ing the executive pastry chef now, not someday."

What I meant was simple yet profound: to reach your next level, you must embody that level in how you present yourself every day. Your posture, curiosity, execution, and leadership—all must reflect who you are becoming.

He took that to heart. Three years later, I ran into him at the Marriott Marquis Hotel in San Francisco, where he had become the executive pastry chef. He had achieved his vision of himself through effort, attitude, and intention.

Leadership Is a State of BE-ing

This approach is based on the BE→DO →HAVE philosophy.

- **BE** a leader (adopt the mindset and behavior)
- **DO** what great leaders do (model, mentor, communicate)
- **HAVE** the impact and influence of a genuine leader

This philosophy applies to every team member, regardless of role. Whether a dishwasher or a department head, the potential for leadership can be developed when individuals learn to lead themselves and support others.

From Head Chef to Head Coach: Changing Leadership Mindsets

In a busy kitchen, clarity, consistency, and care are essential. Early in my leadership journey, I believed my role was to be the expert, to know everything. I personally created each menu, planned every prep list, and handled every issue.

But that approach drained me and limited my team.

Everything shifted when I stopped asking, "What should I do?" and began asking, "How can I make this a team win, and who do I need to BE?"

By shifting from "hero" to "coach," I empowered my staff to recognize their own potential. My role was no longer about directing traffic—it was about inspiring others to lead, think, and act as owners.

A Real-Time Application: Preparing for Valentine's Day

One Valentine's Day, the busiest day of the year, I walked through our team and asked our dishwashers, "How would you plan for this night?"

They immediately suggested a smart plan: hire a short-shifted utility worker whose only job was to make sure silverware and glasses were cleaned and ready for each changeover. That one change reduced delays, pleased guests, and saved thousands in overtime costs. It wasn't my idea—it was theirs.

Why did it work?

Because **leadership was shared**, not kept for the top.

The Six Pillars of Peer Leadership

These are the six leadership traits we fostered in every team member, whether in the kitchen or the boardroom:

1. **Clarity of Vision**

    Great leaders clearly communicate the purpose. They link team members to the "why" behind every task.

2. **Courage to Step Forward**

    Leaders show courage by taking initiative, even when it feels uncomfortable. This involves asking tough questions, offering feedback, or suggesting new ideas.

3. **Consistency in character**

    Leadership is demonstrated, not just stated. Integrity, humility, and personal accountability are what your team sees—and follows.

4. **Commitment to Growth**

    Learning is essential. We motivate our team to set personal growth goals as part of their role development.

5. **Curiosity over Judgment**

    Leaders don't assume—they ask questions. We trained team members to inquire. "What else could be true?" before casting blame.

6. **Care for the Culture**

    Leaders influence culture. Through moments of appreciation, mentorship, and setting boundaries, each person contributes to the team's environment.

The "Act As If" Model

This is where everything comes together: the idea that the quickest way to become the leader you want to be is to **act as if you already are**.

It's more than "fake it till you make it"—it's about aligning neurologically and emotionally. When you think like a leader, speak like a leader, and act like a leader, your environment will start to respond to you accordingly.

It functions at every level.

The Ripple Effect of Internal Leadership Development

Organizations that invest in developing leaders at every level gain benefits:

- Enhanced retention and morale
- Faster decision-making
- Greater innovation
- More robust succession pipelines
- Reduced micromanagement
- A culture of responsibility and ownership

Cooking Team Building as a Leadership Lab

In our TAC™-based Cooking Team Building sessions, we imitate this type of leadership. Each kitchen station becomes a mini-team where members switch roles, share decisions, and take responsibility for the final result.

Through debriefs and guided discussions, participants don't just "do" the task—they reflect on how they **led** or **were led**, and what they would do differently next time.

That's how leadership becomes grounded—through experience, reflection, and integration.

Conclusion: Building from the Inside Out

Leadership isn't about rank; it's about responsibility.

By fostering a culture where each person leads from within—by BE-ing who they're becoming—you cultivate a workforce of highly aligned, fully activated contributors. Whether in kitchens or corporations, that's the recipe for transformation.

Develop leaders. Assemble teams. Observe your organization grow.

Takeaway Recipe

True leadership isn't just a job title—it's a mindset, a model, and a dedication to growth. In this chapter, we discussed how individuals can become the leaders their teams need by embodying the identity and behaviors of leadership today, not someday. We examined the BE ® DO ® HAVE model and showed how organizations thrive when everyone takes ownership of their impact. Whether in the kitchen or the boardroom, leadership is cultivated—not assigned—and it forms the foundation for a sustainable culture. Cooking Team Building isn't just experiential learning—it's a test ground for purpose-driven leadership.

Time to Stir It Up

1. How are you currently *leading* in the ways you want to, regardless of your title?

2. Which of the six peer leadership pillars feels most relevant to you right now? Which one could benefit from more intentional growth?

3. How might your team culture change if every person felt empowered to "act as if" they were already a leader?

CHAPTER 11

EXECUTIVE COOKING — BOARDROOM-READY LEADERSHIP IN THE KITCHEN

"When you recognize people for who they are becoming, you don't just change today, you shape the future."

— *Jim Connolly, CEO Chef*

Chapter Highlights

- Discover how cooking team building offers a unique, high-stakes simulation that reveals authentic executive behaviors in real time.

- Understand why elite leaders must model culture instead of just planning for it—from the boardroom to the kitchen.

- Notice how emotional intelligence, adaptability, and trust become essential when leaders interact directly with their teams.

- Explore genuine executive stories where vulnerability sparked cultural change and enhanced psychological safety.

- Understand how experiential leadership in a culinary setting can drive organizational change that goes far beyond the event.

In a world where executive development often feels sterile—confined to boardrooms, spreadsheets, and seminars—there's a new frontier developing. One where power suits are replaced with aprons, and leadership is not only talked about but experienced in a 95-minute challenge of heat, teamwork, and culinary skill.

Welcome to Executive Cooking

This chapter targets elite decision-makers—CEOs, COOs, Vice Presidents, and Directors—individuals whose influence shapes culture, drives performance, and sets the organization's tone. It invites you to step into the kitchen, not as a gimmick, but as a real-world space for practicing the leadership qualities that today's business landscape demands: adaptive, emotionally intelligent, and trust-centered.

Why Elite Leaders Should Be in the Kitchen

It's common for senior executives to delegate team building. "Send the managers," they say. "My job is strategy."

But leadership isn't just about strategy; it's also about setting an example.

Nothing shows your organization that your personal presence is more important.

When executives work side by side with their teams during a cooking team-building session, something transformative happens. Hierarchies soften, human connections grow deeper, and the leadership behaviors under pressure that usually go unnoticed in the boardroom come to the surface.

One client—a Fortune 100 tech executive—expressed it perfectly:

When my people see me in an apron, not just directing but sautéing alongside them, they understand I'm in this with them. That changes everything.

High-pressure kitchens mirror high-stakes boardrooms.

Great leadership is built under pressure—not polished PowerPoint decks.

In the kitchen, deadlines seem real. The pressure is strong, and feedback comes right away.

Every action, word, and hesitation is amplified.

When executives participate, they do more than just set an example. They experience the same challenges and rhythms that define effective leadership.

We have observed its development:

- The CFO who instinctively micromanaged ingredient allocation as if it were a spreadsheet—until the team stalled.
- The CMO who panicked under pressure—then recovered, regrouped the team, and demonstrated resilience.
- The COO who remained silent for too long—until a single thoughtful question ignited team cohesion.

Every moment reveals executive behavior under stress in real-time, providing insight.

The Key Leadership Behaviors That Develop in the Kitchen

Drawing on over 25 years of leadership facilitation across various sectors, we have identified five executive-level behaviors that emerge during cooking team building.

1. Calm Command

Great leaders manage not only the process but also emotions. When the risotto sticks or the timeline slips, eyes turn to the leader. Your tone sets the mood.

2. **Adaptive Delegation**

   In kitchens, as in companies, control stifles creativity. The best leaders don't just assign tasks—they assign trust.

3. **Vulnerable Visibility**

   Owning a mistake in front of the team? That's not weakness—it's strength. It shows, "You can trust me to be human."

4. **Collaborative Authority**

   Yes, the title matters. But in this kitchen, the real currency is influence. Can you lead even when you're not the loudest? Can you follow even when it's not your idea?

5. **Micro-Moment Awareness**

   High-level executives are often strategic thinkers. In the kitchen, effective leaders also notice the details: the overlooked team member, the unfinished task, the mounting tension. They operate at both 30,000 feet and 3 inches.

Modeling Vulnerability and Trust

During a recent meeting with a global medical device company, the CEO walked in with his sleeves rolled up.

Halfway through preparing, he accidentally burned the sauce—a vital part of his team's dish.

There was a pause, a silence.

He grinned, turned to his team, and said, "Well, that's what I call a prototype."

The room erupted in laughter. What might have been a moment of awkwardness turned into a demonstration of psychological safety.

And here's what happened next: team members who had been quiet started to speak up. They took risks and shared their ideas.

Why?

Because their leader showed that imperfection was not only accepted but also celebrated as part of the process.

That's how vulnerability affects leadership—it unlocks innovation and builds a sense of belonging.

The Executive Who Transformed an Entire Culture

Years ago, we collaborated with an established manufacturing company facing cross-departmental tension. Engineering blamed operations, operations blamed compliance, and compliance blamed leadership.

The new CEO asked to join the team-building event without giving advance notice.

He was assigned to a team of frontline managers—three levels below him on the organizational chart.

He didn't reveal his title.

He listened.

He chopped onions.

He learned the sous-vide technique from a junior engineer.

He served the dessert.

Only at the end—when each participant was asked to share one takeaway—did someone ask, "Wait... are you the new CEO?"

He smiled. "Yes. And I couldn't have had a better first day."

That moment ignited a cultural shift. Teams started working with less fear. Meetings became more collaborative across departments. The story of "the CEO who cooked with us" spread rapidly.

What about the employee engagement survey for next year? The item that showed the most improvement was: *Senior leadership is approachable."*

Why This Chapter Matters

Because culture starts at the top.

Elite leadership isn't just about having all the answers; it's about taking part in the process.

Because the kitchen doesn't care about titles; it always speaks the truth.

If you're a decision-maker seeking your next advantage—not just for your team but for yourself—embrace the challenge.

Put on the apron.

Lead the way.

Share the load.

When you change how you present yourself, your culture will follow.

Takeaway Recipe

This chapter makes a strong case for why senior executives should actively participate in cooking team-building—not just as spectators, but as hands-on participants. By stepping into the kitchen, leaders have a unique chance to demonstrate the behaviors they want to see in others: staying calm under pressure, practicing flexible delegation, showing vulnerability, and being aware of small, immediate moments. These experiences go beyond traditional leadership training by offering real-time feedback, encouraging genuine connection, and creating a shared story that transforms company culture. When leaders choose to approach their roles differently, it sparks a ripple effect across the organization—building trust, breaking down hierarchies, and strengthening team cohesion. The kitchen is not only a metaphor but also a testing ground for modern executive excellence.

◉ Time to Stir It Up

1. When was the last time your team saw you make a mistake, and how did you react? What impact did it have on their trust in you?

2. How might your leadership style shift if your title were invisible for a day?

3. What leadership behaviors do you most want to demonstrate, and how could a high-pressure, team-oriented environment, like a cooking experience, reveal those qualities?

CHAPTER 12

IMPLEMENTATION MODELS OF TAC™

"Recognition isn't a reward—it's a responsibility. When you nurture people's effort, you harvest their excellence."

— Jim Connolly, CEO Chef

Chapter Highlights

- Discover how TAC™—Team Associative Conditioning—goes beyond a single event to becoming a cultural operating system.

- Learn the step-by-step implementation model that begins with cooking team building and expands into leadership development and organizational integration.

- Examine how real-world companies have achieved measurable results in engagement, retention, and collaboration through TAC™.

- Understand the importance of leadership modeling, accountability systems, and strategic rollout in changing workplace culture.

- Gain insights into scaling culture sustainably across departments with flexible, adaptable processes.

Great experiences feel good.

Great systems **influence behavior**.

TAC™ – Team Associative Conditioning isn't just a training method; it's an operating system designed to help companies **reshape their culture** at every level, department, and leadership layer.

In this chapter, we explain the three-phase implementation model that helps teams move beyond "just an event" and achieve complete cultural transformation. Whether you're an HR leader, executive sponsor, or department head, this model is built to scale across your organization.

Phase 1: The Experience — Cooking Team Building

This is the gateway—the spark.

We start with a customized **Cooking Team Building 2.0** event created to:

- Introduce the TAC™ pillars with an engaging, sensory-rich activity that involves high stakes.
- Boost emotional connection, build team trust, and promote real-world collaboration.
- Begin cultivating awareness of leadership dynamics and communication gaps.
- Anchor behaviors through reflection and guided debriefing.

This phase can be a transformative shift for your team. However, when followed by the next steps, it becomes a launchpad.

Real-World Results: Culture Ignited at the Table

A pharmaceutical sales team started TAC™ with a cooking event that exposed significant gaps in their feedback process. Within 30 days, they restructured their feedback system, introduced peer-to-peer coaching, and experienced an 18% increase in team engagement scores.

Phase 2: Leadership Development and Internal Alignment

After the initial experience, we will guide the leadership team into a **training phase** aimed at:

- Establish and develop the four or more TAC™ pillars.
- Help managers incorporate TAC™ into their daily routines.
- Establish internal accountability systems, including communication routines, feedback mechanisms, and role modeling.
- Transition from reactive leadership to **deliberate culture shaping**

This phase generally includes:

- Leadership workshops (either in-person or online)
- Team huddles and habit-anchoring guides
- Accountability checklists for implementing TAC™ in meetings, one-on-ones, and team settings.

Phase 3: Executive Coaching and Organization-Wide Integration

This is the spot where the **long-term ROI** is found.

Integrating TAC™ into the organization's fabric unlocks its true value—retention, psychological safety, agile collaboration, and cultural cohesion.

Phase 3 includes:

- Personal coaching for senior leaders.
- Group coaching for department managers or high-potential leaders.
- Culture audits and action plans

- Company-wide strategic meetings
- Speaking engagements that enhance messaging and unify vision

Real-World Results: Turning Events into Ecosystems

A retail leadership team enhanced their cooking team-building experience with three months of leadership coaching. Their HR Director noted a 23% rise in cross-functional survey scores and a 36% reduction in turnover in the following quarter. TAC™ didn't just strengthen the team—it sparked a cultural ripple effect.

How to Expand TAC™ Across Departments

You don't need to overhaul your entire organization all at once.

TAC™ is modular and scalable.

Here's how companies can grow successfully:

- Start with one pilot department (Sales, Ops, Tech, etc.).
- Identify two to three culture champions within that team.
- Implement the TAC™ phases over 30, 60, or 90 days.
- Use survey data, pulse check-ins, and post-event coaching to refine your process.
- Expand the model to additional departments or business units.

Culture change isn't top-down or bottom-up. It's behavior-out.

Turning Insight into Infrastructure

TAC™ is not just a passing fad. It's a proven, **repeatable model** that develops:

- Deep alignment
- Long-term retention.
- Consistent leadership effectiveness
- A culture that develops under pressure

This shows the shift from cooking together to leading together.

Takeaway Recipe

Turning Insight Into Infrastructure

This chapter has outlined how TAC™ transforms from a powerful team-building experience into a structured model for company-wide cultural change. Starting with immersive cooking team building, organizations activate the emotional and behavioral levers that create trust and cohesion. By layering leadership training and executive coaching, companies hardwire these behaviors into daily operations. TAC™ empowers HR leaders, managers, and executives to replace siloed initiatives with a unified, people-first operating system that scales from pilot projects to full integration. The result? Not just better events, but lasting culture change.

Time to Stir It Up

1. Which phase of the TAC™ model would be the most transformative for your team or department, and why?
2. How can your leadership team use the cooking team-building experience as a launchpad for lasting behavior change?
3. Who in your organization could act as a "culture champion" to help pilot and scale the TAC™ approach?

CHAPTER 13

THE EXECUTIVE PLAYBOOK — SCALING TAC™ ACROSS YOUR ENTERPRISE

"You don't scale a business by adding more people—you scale it by building systems that empower people to lead."

— *Jim Collins, Author of "Good to Great"*

Chapter Highlights

- Explore how the TAC™ (Team Associative Conditioning) model can go beyond individual experiences to promote organization-wide transformation.

- Explore a three-phase approach—**Launch With Impact**, **Scale With Intention**, and **Integrate Deeply**—to embed TAC™ principles throughout your organization.

- Understand the key metrics that matter most to executives and how to demonstrate ROI to gain leadership support.

- See how one tech company used TAC™ to reduce friction, boost engagement, and drive cultural renewal.

- Learn how to develop from a single event into a fully functioning system for culture, collaboration, and performance.

In today's fast-paced business environment, improving just one team isn't enough; you need to align the entire organization around a **common approach to leading, working together, and communicating**. That's where **TAC™— Team Associative Conditioning**—goes beyond the event experience and becomes a **scalable culture model**.

You've seen what TAC™ is capable of in just one Cooking Team Building session.

- Leaders emerge into prominence.
- Communication gets better.
- Collaboration happens more easily.
- A high-performance culture begins to form.

But what if this isn't just a one-time "wow" moment? What if this becomes the **core system for your entire organization**?

Let's show you how.

Phase 1: Launch with Impact — Pilot with Purpose

The journey starts with one cooking experience—but it's never by chance.

In Phase 1, identify your **strategic pilot team**:

- Cross-functional project teams
- Newly established departments
- Leadership development groups
- Change management or culture task forces

Each of these groups offers a high-leverage opportunity to model the desired change. A single experience can **generate quick wins, internal champions, and encourage language adoption** around TAC™ principles.

Sample Timeline:

- **Weeks 1–2**: Align on key behavior objectives such as trust, adaptability, innovation, and others.

- **Week 3**: Carry out your Cooking Team Building 2.0 session with a built-in leadership debrief.

- **Week 4**: Hold a guided follow-up to reinforce key takeaways and pinpoint behavior changes.

Phase 2: Scale with Purpose — From Teams to Divisions

Once the pilot demonstrates success, it's time to expand.

Instead of viewing TAC™ as a one-time training, see it as a **transformational rollout**.

Use internal communication campaigns, department-specific workshops, and executive briefings for:

- Replicate the experience across multiple teams

- Standardize the language of BE-DO-HAVE and sensory-based team learning.

- Establish consistent routines and team cadence

💡 **Key Tip**: Create a "TAC™ Playbook" customized for your organization. Include team debrief questions, behavioral anchors, and follow-up templates.

Phase 3: Deep Integration — Into Culture, Systems, & Strategy

Real transformation happens when TAC™ becomes part **of the organization's mindset and actions**. During this phase, begin embedding the model into:

- **Onboarding programs** (initial experience = cooking session)

- **Leadership development programs** (TAC™ workshops and executive coaching)

- **Quarterly business planning** sessions for team alignment driven by TAC™
- **Recognition programs** celebrate BE-ing and collaborative success.

Corporate Example: One tech company used its TAC™ Cooking Team Building session to kick off a year-long "Culture Reset." Within six months, they reported:

- A 22% increase in employee engagement scores
- 30% decrease in project delays due to cross-departmental friction
- Clearer succession planning emerged as leaders gained experience through shared ownership.

Key Executive Metrics

Executives depend on data. Therefore, give them what they need to say "yes."

Trackable ROI Indicators:

- Engagement and retention metrics
- Project Timelines
- Assessments of manager effectiveness
- Peer feedback scores following TAC™

Example Metric to Share:

Teams that have experienced TAC™ consistently outperform non-trained teams by 18–30% in team-based initiatives over a 90-day period.

From One Meal to Movement

Cooking is just a tool; leadership, culture, and performance are the outcomes.

When you expand TAC™ beyond the kitchen and into your company's ecosystem, you're doing more than just building teams—you're cultivating a **culture of empowered leadership**, prepared for what's ahead.

Now the question is:

Are you ready to lead your organization into its next important chapter?

Takeaway Recipe

Chapter 13 offers a blueprint for expanding TAC™ beyond the cooking event into a scalable system that boosts performance and culture across your enterprise. By intentionally launching pilot programs, scaling with structure, and integrating TAC™ into strategy and systems, companies can transform isolated successes into systemic momentum. From onboarding and leadership pipelines to cross-functional alignment and recognition programs, TAC™ develops into a cultural operating system—not just an experience. The chapter ends with a challenge: moving from one memorable meal to a lasting movement rooted in empowered leadership and collaborative excellence.

Time to Stir It Up

1. Which team or department in your organization would be the best suited to lead a TAC™ initiative?

2. How does your company model and scale leadership, and how could TAC™ improve or speed up that process?

3. What metrics would most persuade your executive team of the ROI of implementing a culture-building initiative like TAC™?

CHAPTER 14

NOW TAKE ACTION—BRING THE HEAT BEYOND THE KITCHEN

> *"Vision without action is merely a dream. Action without vision just passes the time. Vision with action can change the world."*
>
> — Joel A. Barker

You've Prepped. Now It's Time to Cook.

You've explored the principles. You've seen how the kitchen can transform the way people lead, collaborate, and build culture. Now, you understand why team connection, adaptive leadership, and emotionally intelligent systems are not just soft skills—they're crucial survival skills for modern organizations.

But insight alone doesn't lead to change. **Application does.**

This final chapter is your gentle yet direct nudge to move from awareness to action. Whether you're a CEO, VP, HR leader, or culture champion, **you hold the key. Now it's time to turn up the heat.**

Step 1: Reflect—How Does Your Team Truly Operate?

Before diving into the "doing," take a moment to pause and observe. Not just your numbers or strategy—but the human aspect.

- Do your teams have trust in each other?
- Can leaders adapt under pressure without relying on top-down control?
- Are silos preventing real collaboration?
- Does your culture feel stable or conditional?

If these questions make you uncomfortable, **that's a positive sign.** Discomfort acts as a signal—an invitation to explore how Cooking Team Building and the TAC™ framework could help close the gap between where you are now and your leadership goals.

Step 2: Make Team Building a Strategic Priority

If you've traditionally viewed team building as a "nice-to-have," **change your perspective.** As you've seen throughout this book, cooking is more than a meal—it's a high-stakes simulation, a safe container, and a human-powered accelerator.

Imagine if your next offsite didn't just boost morale, but also led to a lasting change in:

- How people communicate in real time
- How Emerging Leaders Take Initiative
- How your teams demonstrate resilience under pressure

Now imagine that change **building up** over time through TAC™: Team → Action →Culture.

That's the ROI that endures forever.

Step 3: Decide—How Will You Use What You've Learned?

Cooking Team Building 2.0 isn't just a concept; it's a commitment to turn moments into action—and action into measurable progress. You don't have to boil the ocean; you just need to light the first burner.

Here are three ways to get started:

1. **Book a Signature Culinary Team-Building Event.**
2. Allow your team to experience the power of immersive learning through a high-trust, high-performance simulation.
3. **Join the Full TAC™ Transformation program.** Use Day One as a launchpad, then grow into executive coaching, group development, and system-wide culture design.
4. **Download our Leadership Toolkit.**
5. Access daily rituals, check-in frameworks, and culture-building guides designed to integrate TAC™ into your daily operations.

You don't need another meeting.

You need **momentum.**

Your Culture Is a Kitchen—Now Lead Like a Chef

Every dish starts with heat and care. So does leadership. It's never just one moment that makes a leader—it's the thousand small adjustments, refinements, and resets that build clarity, trust, and confidence.

The same is true for culture.

Cooking Team Building ignites your passion. TAC™ offers the framework. What will you do next? **That's your legacy.**

Now, move forward.

APPENDIX A - MINI RESOURCE

1. TAC™ Team-Building Conversation Starters

Use these questions during or after your Cooking Team Building event to promote meaningful conversation.

- What did you notice about our team's communication during time pressure?
- "Who stepped up in surprising ways—and what does that reveal about hidden strengths?"
- What similarities can you find between our time in the kitchen and how we function at work?

2. The Three Shifts That Influence Culture-Based Results

This brief guide (available as a one-page document) outlines:

- The shift in mindset: Moving from compliance to commitment
- The behavioral shift: shifting from roles to relationships
- The Leadership Shift: Moving from Title to Impact

Download the one-sheet at: www.ceochef.com/resources

3. Pre-Event Planning Checklist

Before your team's cooking experience, clarify:

- **Objectives**: What is the main result you want your team to accomplish?
- **Participants**: Are there any key dynamics we should be aware of, such as new hires, silos, or leadership transitions?

- **Follow-up Plan**: Will you debrief, coach, or reinforce insights afterward?

Use this checklist to help us tailor the experience—and maximize ROI.

4. Emotional Pulse Tool (Red–Yellow–Green)

A quick tool for gauging psychological safety:

- **Red** = I'm feeling overwhelmed or disconnected
- **Yellow** = I'm uncertain, observing before speaking
- **Green** = I feel safe, energized, and engaged.

Encourage team members to express their "color" during check-ins to foster shared awareness and minimize emotional guesswork.

5 Culinary Challenge Themes to Try

Themes we've successfully used with corporate teams:

- **Fusion Forward** – Innovation Under Pressure
- **Global Market Meal** – Emphasizing Diversity and Inclusion
- **Resourceful Gourmet** – Thriving with Limited Tools
- **Customer-First Feast** – Cooking for an audience or client

These themes directly align with business priorities—ask us how.

6. Invitation to the Discovery Session

If you're still reading, it shows you're committed to building a culture that can grow.

📞 Schedule a 30-minute Discovery Call:

We'll discuss your current challenges and demonstrate how a customized TAC™ experience can help.

🔗 https://calendly.com/jconnolly-1/corporate-cooking-team-building

APPENDIX B – TEAM BUILDING COMPARISON CHART

Experience Type	Immediate Fun	Real-World Transfer	Leadership Development	Emotional Anchor	Lasting Impact
Cooking Team Building 2.0	✓	✓	✓	✓	✓
Escape Rooms	✓	✗	✗	✗	✗
Game Nights	✓	✗	✗	✗	✗
Ropes Courses	✓	✗	✗	✗	✗
Improv Workshop	✓	✗	✗	✗	✗
Sports Leagues	✓	✗	✗	✓	✗
Sports Stadium	✓	✗	✗	✗	✗
Happy Hours/ Social Events	✓	✗	✗	✗	✗
Workshops/Seminars	✗	✓	✓	✗	✓
Volenteering/CRM	✓	✗	✗	✓	✓

APPENDIX C – VARIOUS COOKING TEAM BUILDING THEMES

Here are the top seven most popular programs. All are customized further for your needs. Visit www.ceochef.com

- **1. Corporate Culinary Challenge® (Collaborative)**

Create a gourmet buffet with your team—no recipes, no kitchen, just pure collaboration. This signature program strengthens communication, trust, and leadership through shared culinary execution.

- **2. Ultimate Cooking Championship® (Competitive)**

Bring the heat in our Iron Chef-style cooking competition! Teams battle under pressure in a high-energy, fast-paced culinary showdown that emphasizes strategy, leadership, and creativity.

- **3. Team Tapas™ (Short Format Program)**

Short on time? This 90-minute program delivers powerful team-building through bite-sized creativity. Ideal for conferences, networking events, or leadership retreats with tight schedules.

- **4. Feed the Need™ (CSR Program)**

Give back while building up your team. This heart-centered program combines culinary collaboration with purpose as teams prepare meals for local shelters or community organizations.

- **5. Academic Professional Development Day**

Give back while building up your team. This heart-centered program combines culinary collaboration with purpose, as teams prepare meals for local shelters or community organizations.

- **7. Large Group Cooking Team Building (LGCTB)**

CEO Chef delivers high-energy cooking team-building experiences for 100 to 1,200 participants—turning conferences, summits, and celebrations into unforgettable highlights that inspire connection and teamwork. "Transforming large gatherings into powerful moments of unity and engagement."

APPENDIX D – THE COOKING TEAM BUILDING 2.0 IMPLEMENTATION TOOLKIT: PRACTICAL TOOLS FOR CULTURE CHANGE"

1. Cooking Team Building Planning Template

Purpose: To help HR or event planners clarify their needs and objectives before reaching out.

Contents:

- Team size and location
- Preferred date(s)
- Key training objectives (e.g. collaboration, communication, leadership)
- Event type (Collaborative, Competitive, Short Format)
- Budget range
- Internal stakeholders involved

Why It Matters: Streamlines the inquiry process and encourages alignment among internal decision-makers.

2. Pre-Event Success Checklist

Purpose: A simple page to help clients ensure they've done everything necessary to make the event smooth and impactful.

Contents:
- Confirmed venue & backup plan
- Dietary restrictions collected
- Company culture brief shared with CEO Chef
- Leadership goals outlined
- Participant communication drafted and sent

Why It Matters: Reduces stress and builds confidence that the team-building investment will pay off.

3. Post-Event Reflection Form

Purpose: A printable or digital form teams can use to capture insights and reinforce learning.

Sections:
- What surprised us about how we worked together?
- What did we learn about team roles, communication, or leadership?
- What one behavior will we carry into our day-to-day?

Why It Matters: This form promotes "spaced learning" and reinforces your TAC™ training long after the event ends.

4. Sample Email: Internal Pitch to Leadership

Purpose: Make it easy for your internal champions (like an HR partner or VP) to pitch your services up the ladder.

Structure:
- What Cooking Team Building 2.0 is and why it's different
- A brief quote or stat from your book
- Links to your website or media
- Invitation to schedule a strategy call

Why It Matters: Equips champions with a clear, persuasive case—so you're not relying on their memory alone.

🎯 5. Quick-Start Team Culture Scorecard (TAC™ Self-Assessment)

Purpose: A diagnostic tool to quickly assess how well a team is aligned with TAC™ principles.

Includes:

- Scored prompts under each pillar: Trust, Adaptability, Communication, Action
- Reflection prompts on where improvement is needed
- CTA: "See how Cooking Team Building 2.0 can help"

Why It Matters: Creates urgency and interest to take the next step in your consulting/coaching funnel.

APPENDIX E – FAQ

▪ FAQ: Cooking Team Building 2.0 & The TAC™ Experience

Your Top Questions Answered About the Culinary Team-Building and Culture-Building Process

- **General Program Questions**

Q: How many participants can we include?

We've successfully delivered programs for intimate leadership teams of 8 to large cross-functional groups of 100+. We scale the format to match your space, goals, and timing.

Q: Where do you host cooking team-building events?

We bring the experience to you! We can host events at:

✓ **Your office or corporate space**

✓ **Hotels, conference centers, or off-site venues**

✓ **Commercial kitchens and special event spaces**

If you need help selecting a venue, we can provide recommendations.

Q: Can we do this at our office, or do we need a kitchen?

No commercial kitchen? No problem. We regularly bring our mobile cooking stations to, hotel venues, conference rooms, and corporate offices. We'll help assess your space and recommend the best setup.

Q: How long is the typical experience?

Our core experience ranges from 2.5 to 4 hours. It includes the culinary challenge, team exercises, and a shared gourmet meal. We also offer extended formats with debriefs, keynotes, and custom coaching add-ons.

Q: Do participants need prior cooking experience?

Not at all! No prior cooking experience is required. Our events are designed for all skill levels, from beginners to experienced home cooks. Our professional chefs guide the process, making it a fun and engaging learning experience.

- **Competitive & Specialty Cooking Team-Building Programs**

Q: What is the "Iron Chef: Competitive Cooking Challenge? Our Iron Chef-style competitive cooking challenge is a high-energy, fast-paced team-building event where teams compete head-to-head in a timed culinary showdown. Teams must collaborate, strategize, and create a winning dish to impress our judges!

Q: Do You Offer a Short-Format Cooking Team-Building Experience? Yes! Our Hors d'Oeuvres Team-Building Experience is a quick, impactful 90-minute event—perfect for networking sessions, corporate meetings, or leadership retreats where time is limited.

Q: Can Cooking Team-Building Be Integrated Into a Larger Corporate Event? Yes! Our programs can be integrated into conferences, company retreats, leadership summits, or multi-day training sessions as a fun and engaging breakout activity.

- **Strategic Alignment & Customization**

Q: Can this tie into our leadership, DEI, or sales enablement initiatives?

Absolutely. Many clients use our culinary experiences as immersive simulations to reinforce collaboration, psychological safety, inclusion, resilience, or cross-functional trust.

Q: Can we integrate a company message or theme?

Yes. Whether it's launching a new vision, celebrating a milestone, or aligning around values, we'll infuse your objectives into the team experience—from the welcome message to the final dish.

- **Value & ROI**

Q: What makes Cooking Team Building 2.0 different from other events?

It's not just fun—it's functional. We combine sensory learning, intentional challenge, and structured reflection to create real behavioral shifts. Participants don't just enjoy the meal—they carry insights back to the office.

Q: How Can Cooking Team-Building Activities Benefit My Organization?

✓ Improves **team communication & problem-solving skills**

✓ Strengthens **trust and collaboration** between employees

✓ Encourages **leadership development in a fun setting**

✓ Provides a **memorable, stress-relieving experience** that brings teams closer together

Q: How does this improve team performance?

The act of cooking together activates collaboration, decision-making under pressure, emotional intelligence, and trust—all essential for high-performing teams.

Q: Will we get a debrief or measurable insights after the event?

Yes. We offer facilitated reflection sessions and optional summary reports that link your team's behaviors in the kitchen to real-world workplace dynamics.

- **TAC™ Coaching & Long-Term Support**

Q: What is TAC™, and how does it relate to this experience?

TAC™ (Team Associative Conditioning) is our signature model for sustainable culture transformation. It begins with the culinary simulation and expands into targeted coaching and leadership development aligned with your business strategy.

Q: Can we extend this into a leadership or talent development program?

Yes. Many clients continue with executive coaching, custom group coaching sessions, and strategic consulting to embed TAC™ into their organizational DNA.

Q: What kind of support is available after the event?

We offer a suite of post-event tools, coaching, and team playbooks to help you reinforce new behaviors and sustain momentum over time.

- **Booking & Planning**

Q: How far in advance do we need to book?

We recommend 4–6 weeks for best availability and customization. For urgent timelines, reach out—we're often able to accommodate shorter notice depending on location.

Q: How do I get started?

Schedule a discovery call via www.ceochef.com or contact us at info@ceochef.com. We'll explore your needs and design a program that delivers impact and delight.

ABOUT THE AUTHORS

DR. RENEE GORDON

Relationship Strategist | Speaker | Author | Consultant to High-Performance Leaders

Dr. Renee Gordon is a leading relationship expert and international speaker with over 14 years of experience assisting professionals and leaders in building strong, lasting connections—in business, leadership, and life. Focusing on emotional intelligence, trust-building, and strategic communication, Dr. Renee is recognized for turning the often overlooked "people side" of business into a genuine performance advantage.

Building on her background in advanced human behavior, philosophical theology, and human sexuality, she teaches leaders how to develop meaningful, trust-based relationships across teams, departments, and organizations. She has coached over 2,500 individuals and couples, and now uses that expertise in corporate settings, leadership retreats, and high-level coaching engagements.

Dr. Renee has written several best-selling books, including *Finding Your Love at Last*, *Finding Your Love at Last Duets*, and the international Amazon bestseller *Swipe for Mr. Right*. Her signature process, **Love by Design**™, has helped clients turn friction into flow and build relationships based on mutual respect, shared values, and intentional communication.

She has been featured on *The Doctors*, appeared on the cover of *The New York Times*, and served as a guest expert on several national media platforms. She is also a classically trained chef and former fashion designer—creativity and presence are core elements of everything she teaches and embodies.

Now, along with her husband and business partner Jim Connolly, Dr. Renee uses her relationship expertise in business, leadership development, and cultural change—because in any environment where people work together, relationships are key to growth.

JIM CONNOLLY

Jim Connolly is a high-performance executive coach, team-building expert, and the founder of **CEO Chef Consulting.** For over 29 years, he has helped Fortune 500 companies, mid-sized firms, and mission-driven organizations transform how their teams lead, communicate, and collaborate—using the kitchen as a leadership classroom.

A former executive chef and co-owner of a five-star, Zagat-rated restaurant in Silicon Valley, Jim brings top-tier culinary experience into the corporate world, blending real-time cooking with proven leadership principles. His signature approach has made him a trusted advisor to leading brands like Google, Facebook, Stanford University, Abbott Labs, and Kaiser Permanente.

Jim has also written several business and leadership books, including *Cooking Team Building, How to Access the Hearts of Your Employees by Way of Their Stomachs, iLead, When Will It Be Your Time to Cut Down The Net?*, and his latest flagship book, *Cooking Team Building 2.0*, which redefines team development for today's workplace. Soon after this release, he will introduce his companion guide, *21 Ways to Cook Up Company Culture*—a practical, action-oriented resource designed to turn good teams into great ones by applying the principles from his team-building experiences.

In addition to his consulting work, Jim is a boutique book publisher and book coach who helps speakers, coaches, and business owners write and launch books that position them as category leaders in their field. He is an honors graduate of Johnson & Wales University in Hospitality Management, an

NLP practitioner, and holds a Doctorate in Philosophical Theology. He has been certified by both Tony Robbins & Associates and communication expert Michael Grinder in advanced leadership and group dynamics.

Originally from Providence, RI, Jim now lives in Chattanooga, Tennessee, with his wife and business partner, **Dr. "Love" Renee Gordon**, their cheerful Maltese "Cupcake," playful parrot "Kiwi," and three lively pups: Apollo, Thor, and Zeus.

🔥 Ready to Take the Next Step?

You've just experienced the leadership power of *Cooking Team Building 2.0*. If you're ready to bring this energy into your organization—or help your team apply these lessons every day—here's where to go next:

📔 Coming Soon!

21 Ways to Cook Up Company Culture

The perfect companion to this book—a quick-action guide packed with 21 practical strategies to enhance communication, collaboration, and trust within your team.

Use it with your leaders, share it with your HR team, and foster a strong culture every day, not just at special events.

▶ Available on Amazon and CEOChef.com

🔪 Bring the Experience to Your Team

Want to turn these pages into a real-world experience?

Book a **live Cooking Team Building program** for your next leadership retreat, sales meeting, or culture kickoff.

- ✔ Onsite and virtual options
- ✔ Customized to your team goals
- ✔ High-impact, memorable, and results-driven.

📌 **Visit <u>CEOChef.com</u>** or email *<u>info@ceochef.com</u>* to schedule your session.

📖 Considering writing your own book?

Your book should work as hard as you do. I assist speakers, coaches, business owners, and company leaders in writing and publishing books that boost their credibility, brand, and revenue.

You don't need to be a writer; you need the right strategy.

🔑 Let's talk about how your book can open doors.

⬇ Visit FastBookPublishing.com or connect with me on LinkedIn: *Jim Connolly, CEO Chef*

www.ingramcontent.com/pod-product-compliance
Lightning Source LLC
Chambersburg PA
CBHW050643160426
43194CB00010B/1786